Horse of Fire

The Story of an Extraordinary and Knowing Horse

As told by
JJ Luck

authorHOUSE®

AuthorHouse™
1663 Liberty Drive, Suite 200
Bloomington, IN 47403
www.authorhouse.com
Phone: 1-800-839-8640

First published by AuthorHouse 9/24/2008

ISBN: 978-1-4389-1191-5 (sc)
ISBN: 978-1-4389-1190-8 (hc)

Printed in the United States of America
Bloomington, Indiana

This book is printed on acid-free paper.

Cover Art by: Sabina Turner

Photos by: Kevin Sadler (The Training Regimen), Ira Flushman (Racing Days, A New Home, A Calamity, A Hunting Expedition, Natural Horsemanship), Elyse Ecker (Tristan, Juan), and Lisa Pruitt.

For Savanna

and my extended herd—both equine and human

Horse of Fire

Today the air was thick
Nature was preparing a gift from the spirit world
A young eagle and her vulture companions
soared through the sky
A butterfly flickered through the air
Something was transforming on the horizon
And from the earth a horse of fire was born
The filly expressed her exuberance as she came to life
This fiery chestnut is a spirited creature
of internal beauty and strength
Her long mane flows as she runs through the wind
She is like no other horse
She has the heart of a Thoroughbred
the courage of a war horse
and the stamina of a draught
The eagle and butterfly stay near her
She is guided by the spirit world and will be a healing horse
She will always run wild
sharing her spirit with others but never to be contained
She deserves a name
For now she is known as Fire Horse

TABLE OF CONTENTS

PROLOGUE

Many years ago on a beautiful spring day, April 20 to be exact, a special colt was born into this world. He was bold and charismatic and exceedingly smart. This creature seemed to glow with his fiery chestnut coat and flowing mane. He had been bred to run. His father was a racing horse named Geneo JJ, from the famous Go Man Go bloodline. His mother, Windy's Luck, was also of racing descent, and her lineage included Man of War and Sea Biscuit. This young colt was appropriately named JJ Luck to honor his dam (mother) and his sire (father). With his pedigree, it was no wonder that this young colt would grow up to be a special horse. However, he would not grow up to be a famous racing horse as so many of his ancestors had been. Thankfully for many people in this world, JJ chose a different path.

According to horse astrology, horses born between March 21 and April 20 are Arian horses born under the sign of the Ram. Astrologists say that these horses are seldom appropriate for the novice rider. Often these horses are fiery in both color and temperament — *a horse of fire*. The Arian horse is courageous, with irrepressible energy. They are often ideal as eventers, hunters, or racehorses. These horses like to win, lead, and celebrate in themselves. These horses are not happy being backyard horses, and they won't be happy pulling a clumsy cart, as they know that they are far too special for such a task. If he is not utilized to his potential the Arian horse may become known for his naughty behavior. There will be many times in his life when people will curse this horse. However, it is said that if you can manage this horse, then he will be the best ride of your life.

JJ Luck certainly had all the attributes of an Arian horse. This probably contributed to his short career in racing. He was not fond of the starting gates, and he did not particularly care to have his rear end paddled on racing days. He was also not fond of the daily hot walking practice at the racetrack. JJ would run when he pleased. Other times, if he did not want to run, he would rear, buck, or refuse to move. JJ actually won a few races—when he felt like it—but he soon learned that he didn't care for the sport. JJ was retired at the age of three. A horse that manages to have himself retired at the age of three without injury is a pretty smart fellow.

JJ was sold to a new owner who placed him in a large pasture so that he could recover from his racing career before starting his new career as a jumping horse. He was placed in pasture with a herd of horses. It wasn't the most luxurious life, and it was certainly nothing like his life as a racehorse. When JJ was racing, he had lived in a manicured stall that was bedded with deep, soft straw. He had been fed high-quality grain, and was groomed and exercised daily. At night, when it was cold, he had been blanketed for warmth. He had enjoyed the travel and his fans on the racing circuit. In fact, he had lived like royalty while he was a racehorse. JJ thought back to his racing days and realized that his racing life had been pretty good — well, except for the racing part. JJ had imagined a different life as a retired horse. He had thought that in his retirement he would keep all the luxuries of the racing life — but that was not how his retirement worked.

In his post-racing home, he lived outdoors with a herd of horses in a large, rocky pasture. JJ found himself low in the herd pecking order, and he rarely had first choice of food. Often he grazed on the remaining hay that was left after the other horses were done eating. In this environment, JJ lost his glossy shine and became gaunt, with his ribs protruding under his dull coat. He was often missing his shoes, and the other horses had eaten most of his tail. JJ was horrified when he saw himself in the reflection of a drinking pond one day. He thought, *What has happened to me? I was a beautiful young colt. This wasn't the life I was supposed to have. I am special. Doesn't anyone else see this?* As the year progressed, he found himself quite depressed by the circumstances in his life.

Over the course of the year, JJ was put up for sale. Many people came to look at him. His advertisement described him as a beautiful, bright chestnut with great athleticism. The problem was that when people arrived to see him they saw a young, gangly horse who did not yet have much training or balance. One day a young woman came to see him. Like the others, she noted his gangly experience and imbalance, but she also saw a spark in his eyes and a grace in his movement. She left that day without him, and JJ was heartbroken. *Wouldn't anyone take me home and let me blossom into the horse I was meant to be?* He was discouraged — he had thought there was a connection with that woman. She too was a fiery chestnut and born in the sign of Aries—didn't she know that they were destined to be together? He was sure of it. Weeks went by, and he remained in his pasture with no one to love him. One day his owner placed JJ in the horse trailer. He wondered, *Where am I going now?* When he arrived at the new farm, he was disoriented. *Where am I?* Then JJ saw her—the woman who had ridden him just a few weeks ago. JJ decided to call her Fire Horse. JJ was certain that he and Fire Horse would be together through all of time. She was his destiny, and he would blossom in her care—he knew it. He had come home finally. Fire Horse turned him out into a large pasture, and JJ celebrated. He galloped and bucked in his exuberance—he was spectacular to watch. What follows is the story of this very special horse.

A STAR IS BORN

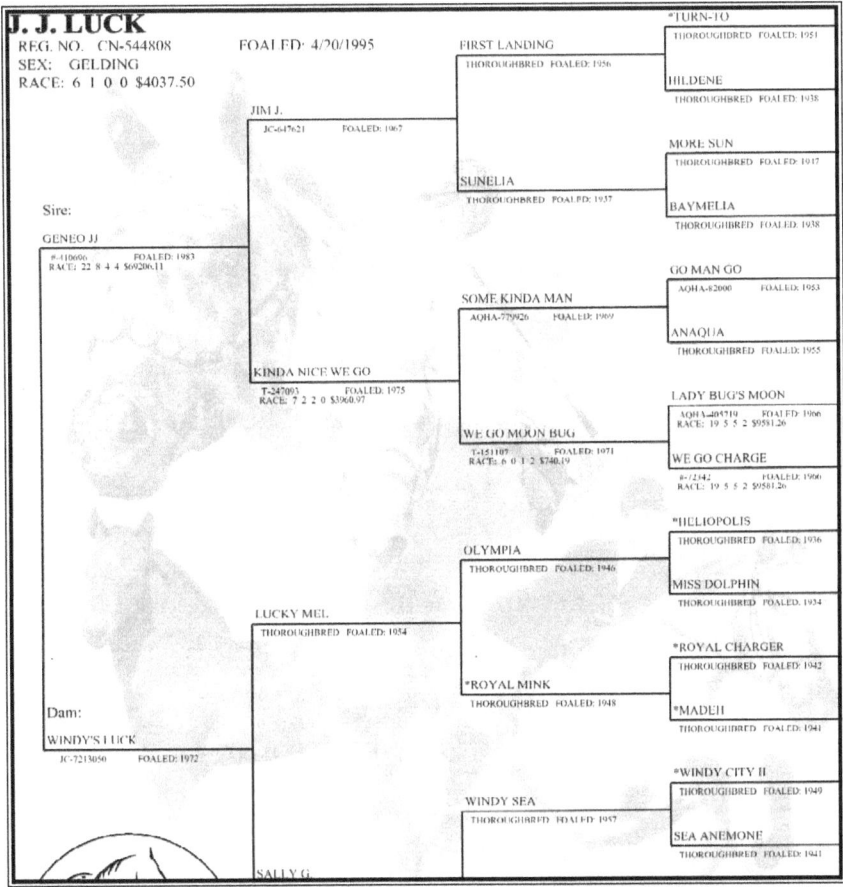

J. J. LUCK
REG. NO. CN-544808
SEX: GELDING
RACE: 6 1 0 0 $4037.50

FOALED: 4/20/1995

Sire:

GENEO JJ
#-116696 FOALED: 1983
RACE: 22 8 4 4 $69206.11

JIM J.
JC-647621 FOALED: 1967

FIRST LANDING
THOROUGHBRED FOALED: 1956

*TURN-TO
THOROUGHBRED FOALED: 1951

HILDENE
THOROUGHBRED FOALED: 1938

SUNELIA
THOROUGHBRED FOALED: 1937

MORE SUN
THOROUGHBRED FOALED: 1947

BAYMELIA
THOROUGHBRED FOALED: 1938

KINDA NICE WE GO
T-247093 FOALED: 1975
RACE: 7 2 2 0 $3960.97

SOME KINDA MAN
AQHA-779926 FOALED: 1969

GO MAN GO
AQHA-82000 FOALED: 1953

ANAQUA
THOROUGHBRED FOALED: 1955

WE GO MOON BUG
T-151107 FOALED: 1971
RACE: 6 0 1 2 $740.19

LADY BUG'S MOON
AQHA-405719 FOALED: 1966
RACE: 19 5 5 2 $9581.26

WE GO CHARGE
#-12542 FOALED: 1966
RACE: 19 5 5 2 $9581.26

Dam:

WINDY'S LUCK
JC-7213050 FOALED: 1972

LUCKY MEL
THOROUGHBRED FOALED: 1954

OLYMPIA
THOROUGHBRED FOALED: 1946

*HELIOPOLIS
THOROUGHBRED FOALED: 1936

MISS DOLPHIN
THOROUGHBRED FOALED: 1934

*ROYAL MINK
THOROUGHBRED FOALED: 1948

*ROYAL CHARGER
THOROUGHBRED FOALED: 1942

*MADLI
THOROUGHBRED FOALED: 1941

SALLY G

WINDY SEA
THOROUGHBRED FOALED: 1957

*WINDY CITY II
THOROUGHBRED FOALED: 1949

SEA ANEMONE
THOROUGHBRED FOALED: 1941

My long legs seemed to be entangled around my ears as I was dropped into this world. I landed on a bed of deep straw and tried to scramble to my feet while my mother nudged me to take my first steps. As I took stock of myself, it seemed that my hooves were an impossible distance away. I staggered as I tried to find my footing in the warm, sunlit straw. After several attempts, I stood tall next to my mother as she groomed me. As I looked at her, I saw that she was absolutely beautiful. She had exquisite long legs and was a bright chestnut in color. Her coat had the color of the setting sun on a hot summer's day. Our coats matched almost perfectly. Her eyes, like mine, were fluid and knowing. I immediately felt her love around me. She welcomed me to this world with her soft nicker. She told me about my lineage and told me that I was named JJ Luck after my parents. The "Luck" part of my name had come from her—her name was Windy's Luck, and she had come from a long lineage of Thoroughbred racing horses, including Man O' War and Sea Biscuit. She told me that they had been legendary horses. I was feeling proud as I listened to her. Then she told me that "JJ" had come from my father, who was a racing Appaloosa. My father's name was Geneo JJ, and he too had come from a long ancestry of racing horses, including Go Man Go. I felt so proud of my lineage and at the same time I felt my feet growing hot under me. Suddenly I felt the need to leap about and celebrate myself. Just as I was thinking that I was destined to greatness—splat—I hit the ground as I lost my footing. My mother looked at me lovingly and gently nudged me back up, and then she informed me that I still had much to learn.

"JJ," she said, "although you will probably race in your early years, I think your life may have a different path. You are a colt born of the Arian sign, and I think you will be too independent and headstrong to be happy as a racehorse. It is not as glamorous as it sounds. Trust me."

I sulked, as I thought I was destined to be a legendary racehorse. I thought I would prove her wrong. I fell deeply asleep and dreamed of all my winning races in the future.

My first few days on the farm with my mother were peaceful. I enjoyed my long naps in the soft green grass under the warm sun. We lived on a sprawling ranch with rolling green hills. My body grew quickly as spring turned to summer. My mother and I were turned out with other mares and their fillies and colts. I finally had someone to play with — hooray! My mother had grown tired of my playful antics, and she was pleased that I had new playmates with whom I could gallop, bite, and kick. I came back to her after my first day of play. I had been bitten and kicked. I had much to learn, she said. I would ask her "What do I have to learn?"

She would nicker back softly, "JJ, you have much to learn. You must learn the ways of this world. You will see."

I sulked off with this bestowed wisdom. I pondered my day. *Why had the young colts bitten me? Why did the fillies kick me? I was just trying to play. Oh well. Tomorrow would be better.*

As the weeks passed, I realized my mother was right. I had learned the ways of the herd. I had learned the signals and body language of my equine friends. I learned that the pinning of the ears and the cocking of a leg was a clue that I was about to be kicked or bitten. I got much quicker at reading equine language, and better yet, I got pretty good at pinning my own ears and cocking my back feet too. I also learned that whoever had the dominant role in the herd got first pickings at the food when it arrived. I thought someday I would lead the herd. But in my early days, I just enjoyed frolicking with my friends. I loved to run and buck with my buddies. I loved the wind in my mane and tail. I loved the freedom. As the months passed, I had grown into the finest and fastest colt in the herd. Finally, I had first choice when the hay arrived to the field each day. Each day I would think, *Life is good.*

As the autumn months settled in around us, we were relocated to another farm. I was fascinated by my new surroundings. There was a buzz in the air. The atmosphere felt almost electric. I asked my mother where we were, and she told me that this was the place where horses learned to race. I watched each day as the horses were "tacked up," which is just an expression that means that the saddles, bridles, and racing gear were put on the horses by the grooms. Each morning, I watched the horses gallop on the nearby track. I was always in awe and imagined the day when I too would be out there—leading the pack.

"That looks like great fun, and I can't wait until I get to race," I declared to my mother one morning.

She solemnly responded, "JJ, you have much to learn. I don't think the racing life is for you, my son."

It seemed that she was always saying that to me. Sometimes I wondered if she would ever have any other words of wisdom for me. I had my own thoughts on the matter. *Someday I would show her that I too was destined to be a great racehorse!*

The darkest day of my life came just a few months later. I was turned out as usual in the large, rolling fields with my equine friends. We were taking our morning naps as we lay in the warm sun. Suddenly I was startled from my sleep by a familiar whinny. Off in the distance, I saw a horse being loaded onto a horse trailer. For a moment, I thought I was mistaken. It couldn't be—it looked like my mother. In an instant, I was up on my feet. As I focused on the horse, I realized that it was in fact my mother being loaded into the trailer. I was filled with anxiety. Adrenaline filled my veins. I galloped as fast as I could to try to reach her.

"Wait for me. Wait for me!" I exclaimed.

She whinnied back to me, " JJ, I must leave you now. Please know that you are a very special horse. I see great things happening in your life. I know that you are destined to find a human who will enable you to blossom in her care. Just trust that she is coming."

Then she was gone. I cried. I whinnied. I bucked. I felt alone in this world for the first time in my life. In my last exchange with her, she finally said something to me besides, "JJ, you have something to learn," and yet clearly I had much to learn, because I hadn't a clue what she meant by her final statement to me.

RACING DAYS

It was early in the morning when I was awakened by a loud noise in the barn. I stirred in my straw bedding and attempted to get some more sleep. I really do enjoy my sleep. The roosters hadn't even crowed yet. What time was it? The commotion was now outside my stall door. My stall door opened. I was barely able to make out the outline of a young man with a halter in his hands. I thought he must be in the wrong barn, and certainly he was at the wrong stall. Didn't he know my routine? Didn't he know that I slept until the morning grain arrived and then I munched on my hay in the warm sunshine out in the large, rolling pasture as I watched the young racehorses being exercised on the racetrack? This man clearly had intentions of having me get up. Finally I relinquished myself to his wishes. Okay. Okay. I wearily got myself to my feet and thought (or hoped) that breakfast was early that day.

It quickly became clear to me, however, that my breakfast would be delayed. I was to be "started" that day. In other words, this was the start of my racing career. When horses are prepared for their various careers, they need to be exposed to the specific tack or harness they will wear in their career. Then they are started on a regimen that prepares them for their chosen career. It is our education system. As the horse is exposed to the will of his owner's wishes, the term is often called "breaking a horse" and, if done incorrectly, that is exactly what can happen. A horse's spirit can easily be lost in the process of being started. Today was to be the first day of my racing career. First, I was led to an area of the barn where I would be groomed. My coat was curried to remove the dirt and mud. Ouch! I found that this process pulled at my fine hairs. Then I was brushed until my coat was glossy and bright. My mane was pulled—I really protested at that one—so that it would be short and even, rather than the wild mane that it had grown to be. I was led to a farrier who put on my first set of shoes. He used hot shoes, and the smoke that permeated my nostrils caused me to pull my foot away. I was quickly reprimanded. *How long was this going to last? When would I get my breakfast?* Once I was fully groomed and shod (had all my new shoes on), I was placed back in my stall. I had never been so happy to see a bucket of oats.

My groom returned for me a few hours later. I assumed he was turning me out to the pasture so that I could play with my friends. But instead, he brought me back to the grooming station. My legs were wrapped to prevent injury. I could sense the tension in the air, and I added to it with my own unease. They placed a leather bridle around my ears and slipped in a cold sliver of metal (the bit) over my tongue. This bit felt terrible in my mouth—I swung my head around in protest. Then, if they hadn't done enough to me already, the grooms strapped a small leather saddle onto my back and cinched up the girth. I was being suffocated. I felt like I had no place to go—except up! I bucked and reared continuously. When I settled down, they resumed the tightening process. I felt more suffocated every time they cinched up that girth. I don't think any of these guys had a clue as to how it feels to have this thing strapped on so tight. I pinned my ears back and give a polite nip to one of the grooms. I wished they could understand me—*Hey, that was tight enough!* They tried to soothe me, but I was now very grumpy. I started to think that maybe my mother had been right. Maybe racing wasn't as glamorous as it had looked from afar.

Once my tack was all in place, I was led to a round pen. A very long lunge line was slipped through the ring of one side of my bit, over my head, and then attached to the other side of the bit. Then I was tapped lightly with a whip to go forward. I exploded. I could not contain my energy any further. I protested as I bucked continuously in the round pen. My trainer remained patient and urged me forward again. Eventually, after what seemed like an eternity to both of us, I trotted and then cantered forward in both directions. At the end of our first session, I was drenched with sweat. He walked up to me and gave me a pat. "Good boy, JJ. This was a good start." I was returned to the grooming station where my tack was removed and my sweat was hosed away with hot water. Then I was turned out with my friends in the pasture. This was a day I would not soon forget. I galloped toward my friends. I had so much to tell them.

As the days progressed, I found myself more amenable to the training process. I no longer bucked or reared. However, I was still not very fond of the early mornings or the grooming process. One afternoon a few weeks later, the routine changed. I was tacked up and worked in the round pen by my trainer, as usual. But then he summoned a young man to climb onto my back—the trainers call this "backing." This frightened me. I bolted from this scary being climbing onto me. But I couldn't shake him, so I bucked him off. The process repeated for hours. Finally, I gave in and let him stay on my back. Once he had secured his position on my back, I was asked to trot and canter. Eventually I settled into my training routine. I had my uncertainties about the process, but I also knew that it was necessary if I ever wanted to be a racing legend like my ancestors had been.

Once my training had begun in earnest, I would often think, *Why do we have to run so early? Couldn't we do this in the afternoon, maybe after lunch?* I often stomped my feet or pawed with my front hooves to express my disapproval to my grooms as I stood in the crossties. It seemed that I was always being curried and brushed. I hadn't seen my mother in several months, and now I was beginning to understand her lack of enthusiasm about racing.

Several months later, I had my first experience on the track. A young exercise rider was placed on my back, and yet

I was filled with excitement rather than fear. My racing trainer stood by our side along the track. The track dirt was packed tightly under my hooves. The air was cool and the morning fog was giving way to the sun rising in the distance.

I heard the trainer speaking to my exercise rider, "JJ is a youngster, but I think he is ready. Try to let him have an easy gallop and feel the track, but don't push him too hard. This horse definitely has racing blood, but he is also quite temperamental. So we'll take it slow in his training."

I felt the adrenaline surge in my veins. I was so excited that I found myself unable to walk. I pranced as other horses zipped by us on the track. I breathed in the adrenaline of all the other horses. It seemed like an eternity and then we were off to the races, so to speak.

I felt my long legs stretching underneath me as we galloped around the track. It felt good to let loose on the dirt. My lungs began to burn as I felt the wind in my face. I was running. I was free. My mother was wrong—I was destined to greatness. I could feel it in my blood. As I surged on the track, I found myself daydreaming. I thought, *I'll probably win the Kentucky Derby some day. I'll be famous like my ancestors have been.* If horses could smile, I would have been smiling in that moment. After my morning exercise, I was given a hot shower and then steamed oats for breakfast. I thought to myself that I liked being a racehorse.

For the next several months, I basked in my training to become a famous racehorse. Then my first race day arrived. We were loaded into starting gates. I had some prior training with starting gates, but I suddenly felt like a stranger to the process. As my grooms led me toward the starting gate, I was consumed by its darkness. I protested. I reared. As a last resort, I whinnied to anyone who might listen, "Why do I have to go in there? Can't we just start the race behind some line? I don't want to load into that starting gate." I was consumed by a group of men who poked, prodded, and spanked my bottom until I was in the confining, cold darkness. I felt the harsh metal on my sides. I could not see anything. It was terrifying. The starting bell rang. All the other horses had exploded from their starting gates, but I was lost in my own fear. I observed the smorgasbord of colors displayed by the jockeys and their mounts. I froze as I watched the group get farther away. Time seemed to stand still as I watched this tumultuous event. The distance between us grew as the pack made their first turn on the racetrack. I watched from afar as though this were a bad dream. Suddenly, the sting of a sharp blow startled me. My jockey was hitting me with his whip with all his might to get me to move. Finally, my feet moved. I scrambled to catch up to the other horses. In short time, I caught up with the last of the pack. The dirt from the hooves of the horses ahead hit my face. My jockey was beating my rear end continuously. I whinnied, "Stop that." *Can't humans understand us?* I tried to buck so that he would get my message. But he hit me more furiously and I fell farther behind. My mind was now consumed with the flogging of my hindquarters by this annoying jockey on my back. *Why does he have to hit me so hard? I can see what place I am in. Hitting me harder isn't going to make me run faster. Did Sea Biscuit have to endure this type of abuse? I think not!* I chose to stop running altogether. I placed last. My mother was right — I hated being a racehorse.

After my first horrific race, my trainer worked with me for the next several weeks on loading into various starting gates until I was no longer bothered by them. In actuality, the starting gates were something that I learned to tolerate, but I was never a fan of being locked into a confining, dark metal enclosure waiting for a bell to ring so that a string of young Thoroughbreds could thunder out at lightning speed.

When my next race day arrived, I loaded nicely into the gate. I was ready. I was thinking, *Kentucky Derby here I come!* I felt great. I felt like a speed machine. My legs were made for running! The bell rang and we burst out of our starting gates. I could see my competition as we all scurried through the pack to get a lead position. I was stuck in the middle of the pack. I really needed to have a better start, because I truly hated having dirt thrown in my face. The view was always much better in the front. I saw my opening and my jockey guided me tightly on the inside turn. I took the lead. *Ah, this was much better.* I could see now. I could feel the horses around me and behind me. Our hooves were thundering in the dirt. Our nostrils flared and we sounded like speeding trains as we headed around the track. I was now in the lead, but I sensed that another horse was catching up to me. I was not going to lose this race. I gave it all I that I had. I won! I loved being a racehorse!

Soon after my first victory, my opinion of racing was permanently altered. It had been a cold, wet day. I was not racing that day and was rather enjoying my leisure time in the grassy pasture overlooking the race field. I heard the starting bell. I heard the thunder of hooves. I absorbed the roar of the crowd as they cheered with excitement. I munched on my sweet grass. Then the air became still. I suddenly felt anxious. I looked back down at the racetrack. The thundering herd had become one large mass. Only the lead horses had managed to escape the pile-up. The crowd had grown silent. I moved closer to get a better look. Slowly the horses and their jockeys got up from this chaotic heap. I saw various gashes and injuries bestowed upon both humans and equines alike. To my horror, one jockey and mount did not get up. Two ambulances arrived: one for the rider and the other for the horse. I wasn't sure of the fate of either being, but it made me realize immediately the danger of this sport. One misplaced foot could cost us our lives. I found this ominous event had a profound effect on me — I no longer wanted to race.

The next several months were challenging for me. My enthusiasm for racing had been diminished by my observation of the racing accident. My jockeys were constantly whipping my rear end with their crops on race days. I managed to place in the top three in a few more races, but I had grown tired of the other side of racing. Something had shifted in me. I had an underlying fear about the danger of the sport. I did not like getting up at four in the morning for six days a week so that I could be groomed and exercised. I did not like being tied to a hot walker, which is a mechanical contraption that a horse is attached to so that he can be walked for a few hours each day. It was on this contraption that I learned to throw my head, as I would throw my head continuously in protest to this process. On racing days, I did not enjoy having my rear end paddled with a crop, and I certainly did not like "not winning," as I really did not like dirt kicked in my face. As time progressed, I found this life very stressful. I was often sore and tired. Most days, I really just wanted to go out to the pasture and take a long nap. Maybe my mother was right. Racing was not the glamorous life that I had imagined it to be. Maybe I was not cut out to be a racehorse.

As my desire to be a great racehorse dwindled, I found myself less enthusiastic about racing. I hadn't won a race since my first day, and I had shown in only a few other races, but even those victories seemed a thing of my past. My enthusiasm was gone. As a result of my poor racing performance, I was gelded. This was not a pleasant experience and more importantly, it ruined my opportunity of living a lush life as a stud horse. I was to be sent to the auctioneers to be sold. I was only three years old, and my first career was already over. I hadn't given up, however, as my mother had told me that I was destined for a great life outside of racing.

A NEW CAREER

It was auction day. I had hoped that my mother was right and that my special human was going to buy me today. All of us were placed in a holding bin with numbers painted on our sides. There was nothing glamorous about this process. When my number was called, a handler brought me into a large arena filled with people. I heard myself described to the audience by an auctioneer. I liked hearing his words. "Well, folks, here is a special young horse. His racing name is JJ Luck out of Geneo JJ and Windy's Luck. This horse has great pedigree: Go Man Go on his dad's side and Sea Biscuit, we all remember Sea Biscuit, and Man o' War on his mom's side. This colt will make a great hunter, jumper, or three-day-event horse. Just look at his legs, folks. Those long legs were meant for jumping. Look at this youngster. You can see the intelligence in his eyes. Look at this magnificent chestnut colt. He is three years old and ready to be your greatest show horse," he exclaimed to the audience. I pranced around my handler as I heard these words. I thought, *I am a magnificent horse! I just wasn't cut out for racing but I am sure I can be a great hunter or jumper or three-day-event horse – whatever that means.*

The auctioneer started the bidding. I don't think I have ever heard numbers rambled off so quickly. My heart was racing. It seemed more chaotic than my experience with the start gate at my first race. He bellowed off to the audience, "We'll start the bidding at five hundred dollars. I see five hundred dollars (a woman in the audience held up her hand), how about six hundred dollars, folks?" This process continued for what seemed like an eternity and finally I heard that I was "sold to the man in the back row for three thousand dollars."

I panicked as I looked up at the man in the back row and then back at the auctioneer. My mind was racing. *There must be some mistake. I am not supposed to be bought by a man. It has to be one of the women in the audience. My mother clearly said to me that it would be a woman who would come into my life and let me blossom.*

After the auction, I was loaded up into a large trailer by this man. He had a quiet disposition about him, and he seemed to have much horse experience. He calmly guided me to the front of the open stock trailer. I was alone in this large, open vessel. I stomped and whinnied in protest. I was given a flake of hay to munch on – a "flake" of hay is actually much larger than it sounds - it is about five pounds of hay. The trailer pulled out of the auction grounds, and we seemed to drive for days, although I think it was just one long day. When we arrived at our destination, it was dark. I was led to a large field that was fenced in with barbed wire and a large metal gate. The gate was opened, and I was brought into the pasture. Another flake of hay was dropped at my side. Then I was left in total darkness as the truck and trailer drove away.

"Wait, come back. There is some mistake! I sleep in a stall! You can't leave me here out in the cold with no blanket. Didn't you hear the auctioneer? He said I was a magnificent colt with great promise as a show horse. Where are my steamed oats? Come back!" I exclaimed to him as I whinnied frantically in the darkness. It was of no use. The lights from his truck and trailer disappeared as he drove away from the ranch.

I was now standing alone in the pitch black of the night. The adrenaline surged in my body. At first I was filled with panic, then abandonment. I felt much like I had on the day I had been separated from my mother. I was alone and scared. I didn't know where I was, and it was ominously quiet. I had never slept outside of a stall or outside without shelter. I searched for a pleasant thought to distract me, but I couldn't find one. At least I had some hay to nibble on. Then I heard something in the distance. *Who is there?* At first I thought it might be a wild animal stalking me. I stood quiet and listened intently. Then I heard a distinctive sound. Clip clop clip clop clip clop ... Then this echoed through the surrounding canyon. It seemed to be getting louder. Suddenly I realized that it was a herd of horses coming my way. I thought this would be great—I'd have some new friends. Then, without warning, I felt the sting of a hoof land on my hindquarters and then another and another. "Ouch!" I whinnied. I tried to defend myself, but I was clearly outnumbered and not welcomed into this group. Suddenly I felt like I had as a young colt when I did not yet know the ways of the herd. Clearly, my mother had been right, I still had much to learn. I decided that it would be best to find another place to sleep. I would have to make friends with these new horses in the morning. As I made some distance between myself and this group of intimidating equines, I could hear them munching on my hay. I found a quiet spot under some trees, and I shivered myself to sleep.

Morning came quickly, but the fog that nestled into the rolling hills had settled into my bones. I felt chilled. In the morning, I spotted a man with a wheelbarrow filled with hay. I thought, *Excellent, here comes my breakfast*, but then I heard it again. The "clip-clop" of hooves that were not mine. Then I saw the herd of horses that had taken my hay last night. I had hoped that things would be different in the morning. I had hoped that I would introduce myself and it would be just like the old days with frolicking friends. Well, I was wrong. I was not invited into this herd. Again I found myself the recipient of pinned ears and cocked legs and the sting of someone's hoof on my backside. *I would starve at this rate.* I tried to find an opening in the herd, and finally I was greeted by an elder gelding who was a steel gray color. He was enormous. He softened his ears and his stance and allowed me to share in his pile of hay.

"Thank you so much," I exclaimed in my high-pitched whinny.

He nickered softly into my ear, "Just eat, my son, so that you have a chance with these bullies."

As the months followed, I learned that my friend who had shared his hay on the first day was a retired draft horse. His name was Remington, "Remy" for short, and he had spent his life pulling carriages. I think the reason he fared so well in this boisterous herd was that he had an enormous presence, and he had the respect of all the horses in the herd. As unruly as they could be, they always yielded to his presence. I grew to admire this wise soul. Remy would not play with me, and he explained he had grown too old for that, but he did spend much time with me sharing his wisdom. I did manage to find some playmates in the group, and it was great to play each day, but I always had my meals and quiet time with Remy. He reminded me of my mother. He too told me, "JJ, this will not be the last place where you live, for I know that you are destined for a different life." Just as before with my mother, I still did not know what this meant. I pondered, *How do some horses just seem to know these things?*

Remy would often say to me, "Just trust in the divine wisdom of the great spirit and you will do great things with your life."

I nickered back to him, "But I would just be happy to hang out here with you for the rest of my life."

Remy whispered to me that his days were numbered and that I would be moving on from this herd shortly. I found myself filled with sadness at the thought of losing another great being in my life and yet curious to know where my life might lead me next.

The next morning, I found myself in a new training regimen. Normally this might frighten me. But I found Remy's words in my heart. A cheerful young woman, who informed me that I was about to embark on a jumping career, greeted me. I sensed her excitement, and I matched it. I started leaping off the ground as I saw the jumping arena ahead of us. Somehow she didn't appreciate my exuberance. As we walked down the path leading from the rolling pasture down toward the main barn, I saw an enormous arena filled with all sorts of intimidating objects. My eyes widened, and I started to shy away. She reassured me that these were just "jumps" and that I would enjoy learning how to jump such obstacles. I was not so sure about this.

I was tacked up by a young groom and then placed in the arena with these scary-looking objects. *I hoped they didn't bite too!* There were two people in the arena, and they started to chase me with long whips. The only way to get away from them was to go over these jumps. I saw the first jump approaching quickly. Panic set into my mind. *What do I do?* But before an answer could come to me, I heard the crashing of wood as I knocked the jump over and galloped around the arena. *Ouch!* The next jump was not going to bite me like that again. As I approached the next jump, I leaped over it like a frightened deer running from a pack of hunters. There seemed to be some exclamation of glee from my human observers. Maybe I was supposed to leap over these rather than knock them down. Jumping wasn't so scary once I realized I was supposed to jump over the obstacles rather than run through them. In fact, I found this sport to be quite fun. For the next few months, I was schooled in various grids of obstacles. I learned in this process that I was very fast and I could clear great heights. I also liked to jump out of the arena any time I was left unattended. I was thoroughly enjoying such freedom!

Just as I was settling into my new training regime, I learned that I would be leaving this farm too. I had overheard my grooms talking about me. They said that I was to be placed up for sale and that my owners were hoping to get a good price for me with my pedigree and jumping ability. I knew these words all too well. It seemed that just as I was getting comfortable in my surroundings I would be plucked away. I said my farewells to Remy as I shared the news. But his response was quite optimistic. "Cheer up, son. You are still a youngster and you have a wonderful life ahead of you. Just trust that this is part of your journey," he nickered wisely. I nuzzled him in gratitude. I would miss this wise soul.

Over the next few months, many people came to look at me. Some would ride me and others would look me over and just walk away. I overheard a few of these people say to the owner that I wasn't worth the money that was being asked for me. I was heartbroken. *What do they mean I am not worth the money? Doesn't anyone see my true value?* But that same day I saw my reflection in the pond as I walked by. I don't think I had ever noticed this before or else I had always thought the reflection belonged to someone else. My first thought was that this mirror image could not be me. I played and danced with this reflection. In fact, it was me! I was horrified! *What had happened to me?* The horse that looked back at me from the pond's surface was emaciated and his coat was dull. He was missing half of his shoes and it looked like his tail had been eaten. *What had happened to that beautiful young colt with the bright chestnut coat and the spark in his eye?* I sought out my friend Remy. I asked him what had happened to me. Remy replied wisely, "JJ, my dear boy, this is all superficial.

Just a little bit of attention, grooming, and some extra food and you will be your old exuberant self. Just trust me. The right person will come along and see your inner beauty and talents. Besides, you don't want to head down the path with anyone who can't see what a beautiful horse you are. You are worthy of the person that sees all of you without judgment." I wondered if this could possibly be true.

The next day my owner and two other women met me at the pasture gate. One of these women had hair that matched mine. She too was a fiery chestnut. I immediately liked her energy and felt a connection with her. I knew in my heart that she was my destiny, and I decided to call her Fire Horse. She smiled at me and then pointed out to my owner that it looked like I had lost my shoes, and that someone had eaten my tail, as well as my fair ration of food. I liked her even more as she pointed out that I wasn't getting the care that I needed. Fire Horse took me down to the round pen and asked if she could see me move freely without my tack. I moved around the round pen with exuberance. I offered my best trot and canter and made the best of having only two shoes on my feet rather than four. Fire Horse said that she really liked my movement and that I seemed to float over the ground. She then asked if she could ride me. Her trainer insisted that she ride me first. I didn't care for that part. The trainer told Fire Horse that I was still quite unbalanced and that she should be careful riding me. But Fire Horse climbed on me anyway. We floated around the arena, and I was so excited that I became a bit high-spirited. I think I may have scared Fire Horse, but I didn't mean to. When she got off me, she gave me big pat and a horse cookie as a treat. I was ready to pack my bags and go home. But then in horror I heard Fire Horse say, "JJ is a beautiful mover, and I really like him. But I think I am looking for a horse that is a bit older and more experienced. Also, I think JJ may be priced too high given that he is only four years old, is underweight, and is lacking in training." She then thanked my owner for her time and drove off in a truck with her trainer. I was brokenhearted.

Over the next few weeks, I found myself quite depressed. I couldn't eat. Remy sought me out one afternoon and said to me with his wise nicker, "JJ, Don't let this get you down. It will all work out. Things happen for reasons that we often don't understand until sometime down the road." Then Remy shared a bit about his own life experience with me, "JJ, I too have experienced things I didn't understand at the time that they were happening. But through my life, I learned that every event in my life had a purpose and actually brought goodness into my life. For instance, at the peak of my carriage-pulling career, I was sold to an older gentleman. At the time, I thought that this was the worst thing that could possibly happen to me, as he wouldn't have the energy to care for me. But when I arrived at his farm, his two young granddaughters greeted me. I was loved and cherished in my new home. His grandchildren groomed me daily. They took me for long rides in the soft grass, and I made sure that they were always safe when they were in my charge. They loved me and treated me like royalty. It was such a wonderful retreat from my carriage days. I grew to love that family dearly, and I lived with them for many years until the older gentleman passed away last year. Again, I thought this would have a terrible outcome. I could have been auctioned off or worse yet sold as meat.

Instead, his passing was the opening of another door in my own life. He had left it in his will that I was to be placed out in pasture upon his passing. I was retired here last year, and it was his will that I live here for the rest of my days. So, JJ, just trust that this unknown journey will work out for you too." I listened half-heartedly. I thanked Remy for his wisdom, but then I isolated myself under the trees in the pasture, and I sulked, as I wasn't so sure that it would in fact work out for me.

A NEW HOME

The next morning my owner met me in the pasture and placed an old halter on me. Then she led me down to a large trailer parked by the arena. It became clear that she was taking me somewhere. "Where are we going?" I nickered. I hadn't been in the trailer since the day I was auctioned from the racetrack. I ate my hay nervously as we drove along the windy road. This drive was much shorter than the last one, and within an hour we had arrived at our destination. The trailer doors opened and I stepped down cautiously. I looked around. There were many arenas, pastures, and horses around the property. I was a bit nervous. But then everything changed. There she was—Fire Horse! She walked over to me and gave my owner a check and thanked her for bringing me over — she told the owner she would give me a good home and that would compensate for the lack of funds she was handing over for me. Then Fire Horse said to me, "JJ, we are going to have a wonderful life together." She turned me out in the arena so that I could stretch my legs. I galloped and whinnied with all my might. I was excited to finally be home.

That first night Fire Horse placed me in a stall, much like the one I had when I was a racing lad, except that this was bedded with shavings rather than straw. She tossed me two large flakes of hay and gave me some grain. I had an enormous water trough in my stall filled with fresh water — which I would splash in when I needed some entertainment! *Life would be good again*, I thought to myself.

The next morning came, and again I was treated to more alfalfa and grain. Best of all, no one would steal hay or food from me in my stall. I was turned out for playtime for a few hours and then returned to my stall. All day I waited for Fire Horse, but she didn't come. But then at last she arrived in the evening. She took me from my stall and turned me out in the round pen. Again I was able to express my exuberance to her. I trotted to the left and to the right and then cantered for her. She smiled at me. When we were done, she gave me a bag of carrots as a treat. *This is a good life*, I thought to myself.

As the days went on, I grew more and more restless. The stall was too confining. I splashed in my water trough to see if someone would come and let me out. But instead I was scolded for making such noise. Not only was I growing restless but it was also hot, and I was growing very itchy in my shavings. When Fire Horse arrived, she took me from my stall. She had a look of apprehension on her face. She was inspecting me and all my itchy spots. She said to me, "JJ, you poor thing. You have hives all over your body." She called a vet and he gave me an injection and prescribed a round of medication and daily baths for the next week. I have never been particularly fond of baths. If bathing was an acquired taste, then I had yet to acquire it. I expressed my opinion and disapproval of this daily bathing. I fussed in the wash rack. Fire Horse was probably wetter than I was at the end of each bath, and she looked as displeased as I felt.

At the end of the week, the prognosis was that I was allergic to something in the shavings, and Fire Horse requested that I be placed out in one of the pastures. I was a bit nervous about this given my last experience with a herd. This experience wasn't much better. I was placed out in a large pasture with three large horses. There was a large black horse, a large white horse, and a small brown (bay) horse. I never had a chance to meet the bay or the white horse. However, I was "greeted" by the large black horse. He obviously did not like redheads, or retired race horses, or horses younger or smaller than himself. I seemed to fit all of these characteristics. Before I even had a chance to introduce myself properly to the herd, I was kicked in my chest and sides, and then bitten on my rear end and spine. "Ouch," I whinnied. Again I retreated to a distant spot in the pasture. This time, however, there was no Remy to shelter me from the bullies. I still was underweight and had no chance against these muscular brutes. I feared that this was not going to be a good situation. Without a friend like Remy in the pasture, I would not stand a chance.

When Fire Horse saw me, she was appalled. She treated my wounds and then asked the owners of the ranch if I could be placed in a "kinder" pasture. It was decided that I would go and live out with a group of older and kinder horses. I am sure this must have seemed strange to place a four-year-old out with retirees. But this was where I needed to be. I was thankful that Fire Horse was looking out for me. I felt safe in her presence.

BLAZE

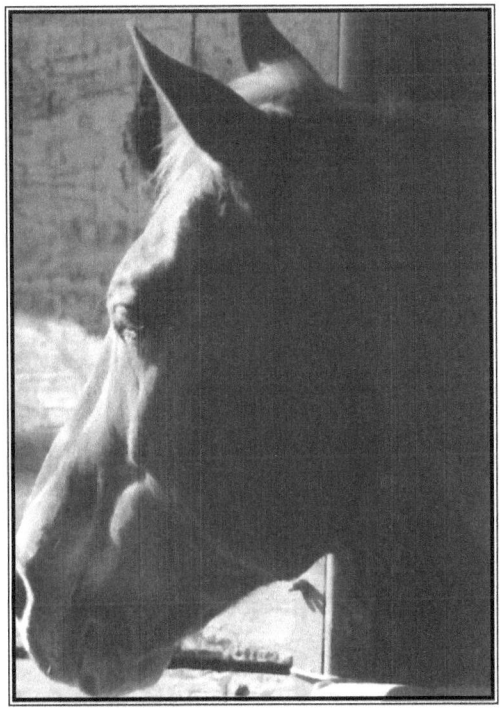

In this kinder pasture I met another horse that also belonged to Fire Horse. His name was Blaze. He was much older than me, had a kind disposition, and seemed wise like Remy had been. Blaze was a large Quarter Horse who, like Remy, had lived a colorful life. Blaze and I spent much time together in the pasture. I had told him of my experiences on the racetrack and then how I was auctioned off to my last home prior to meeting Fire Horse. One afternoon, he shared with me the story of his life.

"I was born in May under the sign of Taurus. Horse astrologists say that a horse born in this sign will be a dependable, placid, and affectionate horse. We are said to be horses that love to be touched and groomed. The Taurus horse is also noted to be very food-focused. We like the reassurance of our herd or family. It is said that we need to feel secure and that we like the reassurance of a predictable routine. I think that I have many attributes of the Taurus horse.

"When I was a young horse, I lived on a sprawling cattle and sheep ranch in snow country. I am a foundation Quarter Horse who was bred to be a working ranch horse. I was brought up to learn the skills of moving cattle and sheep over several hundred acres. My owners were always very kind and gentle with me. I lived that life for several years until an accident changed the course of my life. One afternoon, an old ranch hand took me out to look for the source of stock loss on the ranch—he had suspected that it might be a pack of wild dogs on the upper ridge of the ranch. He saddled me up, and we headed off. I noted that he was wearing his gun across his back. When we reached the peak of the ridge, he saw a group of his sheep by the main creek running through the property. He decided that he would investigate, and he tied me to a large oak tree. The old rancher seemed to be gone a long time. The day gave way to nightfall, and I patiently waited for the old rancher. Then without warning, I sensed something was very wrong. Suddenly I was being attacked by a pack of wild dogs. They had approached me from behind. My flight instinct took over and I kicked with all my might. I pulled as hard as I could to try to free myself, but I could not break free from the tree, and finally my halter broke. I scrambled to free myself from the attack of the vicious pack. In that same instant, a loud shot echoed though my ears. His blast had scattered my attackers. The old rancher probably saved my life.

"I don't know all the details, but shortly after this incident my owners opted to sell their ranch, and their horses. I, too, was sent off to a local auctioneer. One snag in my sale was that I no longer tied. As a result of this terrifying experience, I found myself filled with fear every time I was tied to something. A very nice couple that owned a small horse ranch in another state purchased me. They had a young daughter, and they thought I would be a gentle horse for the family. In their care, I was exposed to many things. The father tried competing me in cutting and reining while the mother competed with me in dressage. The little girl just liked to play games with me, and she often invited the neighborhood children to play games with us as well. I was the most sought after mount of the neighborhood children, who liked to play the red light/green light game. In this game, the leader would not face us. He would say green light, and we could move forward, but when he said red light, we had to stop immediately. When he turned around, if we were still moving, we were eliminated. The first pair to cross the finish line would win. I was quite good at that game, and I can't think of a time that I ever lost! I loved the neighborhood children, and I often took them for bareback rides around the property. I lived with that family for many years. Then one day, the family had traveled out of town. I was left behind and in the care of a new ranch hand. They had forgotten to tell him that I could not be tied to anything. The instant that I would feel pressure on the halter, I would pull back with all my might until something gave way — this could be a fence, a halter, or even a wall of a building. It was the joke in my family that if I were tied to a barn, I might tear it down if I panicked. Their solution had been to ground tie me — essentially, they dropped the lead of the halter where they wanted me to stand, and I had always been happy to oblige. This poor ranch hand didn't know about my 'little peculiarity.' One afternoon he had tied me outside the barn. All was fine until a dog ran behind me and startled me. I pulled back, felt the pressure on my halter, and then pulled with all my might. I was tied with a cowboy halter that wouldn't yield. I pulled until my foot slipped, and then I found myself upside down. This was quite a spectacle, as one can imagine, for I am the size of a draft horse. The ranch hand came running and cut me free, but I was in much pain. I could barely walk. He called my family and told them what had happened. They told him to give me an anti-inflammatory. When they returned a few days later, I was still lame. Over the course of the year, nothing much improved. They tried numerous vets and ailments to try to relieve my pain, but I was not serviceably sound unless I had been given a large quantity of horse aspirin (Bute). The veterinarians advised my family that my best bet would be to find a home where I could live out in a large pasture. Unfortunately, the way their farm was set up, they had two arenas and many stalls, but there was no pasture that I could live on if I remained in their care. They started to look for a new home for me. Many people came to look at me, but my family wouldn't relinquish me to just anybody. So many interested parties were turned away. Then one day, a young woman with chestnut hair came to look at me. I felt the compassion in her heart as she looked at me. I had been given a fairly large dose of Bute so that she could ride me. We got along well, and she rode me beautifully. The family explained my situation and asked that she come ride me several more times in their presence. They wanted to make sure that I was going to the right home. After a few weeks, they decided that she was going to be a good match for me. Best of all, she could offer me a life in pasture. So that is how I came to live here in this pasture. I might add that soon after Fire Horse took me in, she found me a chiropractor — a true horse doctor. In short time, he was able to free up all the joints that I had injured in my pullback accident. I have been sound ever since. So I can tell you, JJ, that Fire Horse is a kind woman with a strong horse spirit. I think we shall both benefit by belonging to her."

As I listened to Blaze's story, I realized that he was a very kind horse, much like Remy. But I also I sensed a bit of jealousy brewing in me. Fire Horse and I were kindred spirits, and while she might also own Blaze, I knew I was her "special horse."

THE TRAINING REGIMEN

Over the next few weeks in my new home, I learned that Fire Horse had aspirations of three-day eventing—in which rider and horse would compete in dressage, cross-country jumping, and stadium jumping—and I was to be her horse. I knew I was destined to be her special horse! For weeks, Fire Horse had been ridiculed for spending money on me. I often heard people at the barn say all sorts of cruel things about me. They often snickered as we walked by and would add comments such as, "Don't you ever feed that horse?" or "He looks like a paper horse—if he turned sideways, he would disappear." One man actually said to Fire Horse, "I can't believe you wasted your money on that horse." Fire Horse always defended me. She would kindly respond, "JJ will fill out—you'll see. He'll be a great horse!" It was nice to have someone who believed in me. Fire Horse brought her parents and her sister up to meet me. *Did that make them my family too?* She put me in the round pen, and I showed off all my paces for them. "He is beautiful, and he is definitely your special horse," Fire Horse's family exclaimed to her. Her family had only kind words to say about me, and best of all, they always brought me wonderful treats. I loved my new family.

When Fire Horse first rode me, I was quite exuberant. Maybe I was a little too exuberant, because all of a sudden she wasn't on my back anymore. I guess I had bucked a little too hard. "I am sorry," I wanted to say as she brushed the dirt off herself. She didn't look very happy about this! In the beginning of our lives together, it seemed that every time Fire Horse got on me, I became electric and somehow we parted company. She was a good rider—it wasn't that—but I do think I could have had a career as a bucking horse! When we would jump obstacles, I often bucked in celebration afterward—but Fire Horse didn't always hang on for the full party. It didn't take very long and I found myself being ridden by trainers instead of Fire Horse. She would come and watch me being ridden by the trainers. Everyone told her I had great jumping potential, but Fire Horse didn't seem to be very happy that she wasn't the one on my back and honestly, I wasn't either. I found myself being worked with strong legs and hands, and my body began to get sore. I was subjected to several days a week of "dressage," which felt like punishment to me. Dressage is word for training that originates from the French. It is meant to describe the formal development of a horse and his muscles so that he can work in a collected frame and have the strength to be in self-carriage. This process typically takes years, but many people try to push the young horses too quickly, and they can become quite sore and resistant.

Over several months, I found myself very tired and sore. I began to resent my training regimen. Fire Horse had me out in pasture, which helped with my flexibility, and she would often bring a massage therapist or chiropractor to work on me—the same ones who worked on Blaze. I did enjoy that. As my training progressed, however, Fire Horse found me elusive and difficult to catch. I wasn't avoiding her; I just did not want to go down to the arena and be ridden by trainers anymore. I wanted her to ride me.

Eventually Fire Horse started to ride me more—although she was always under the discerning eye of a trainer. There was always so much tension and negative energy when we were in the presence of the trainers. They often criticized her in how she rode me. I was happiest when we were just left alone. I often wished we could just go out together and run free without any rules about how I had to be collected, bent, or packaged. I knew Fire Horse was frustrated, and then trainers began to tell her that she should just sell me and get a less "complicated" horse! *What?* Fortunately, Fire Horse was defiant. She explained that I wasn't going to be sold—she was committed to me. Fire Horse switched trainers (at some point I think I lost track of how many trainers I actually had), and we started to work on my jumping—I liked that!

One spring day, I think a year or so after Fire Horse first found me, she took me out for a "cross-country day" with one of her new trainers. Blaze came with us and was ridden by the trainer. He was essentially coming along to be my babysitter. Fire Horse and I had the chance to gallop the fields and to jump all sorts of obstacles together. I loved the challenge of the jumps and the freedom under my feet as I galloped in the open fields. I could feel the freedom that Fire Horse felt too. I think we were both smiling. Then something terrible happened. We were on our final jump. It was a water jump that required that I drop about three feet off of a ledge into a large pool of water. I panicked. I didn't know what to do. Fire Horse urged me on and told me I could do it. I had no idea how deep this water was. *What if we drowned?* To reassure me, the trainer walked in from the other side atop of Blaze.

He nickered, "JJ, it is ok, it is not too deep."

Eventually after a little more urging, I think I belly flopped into the water. When I landed, she gave me a big pat on my neck — but in that instant I had thrown my head up out of fear. Unfortunately, I hit Fire Horse square in the face with the back of my head — I hadn't meant to hurt her. She flopped onto my neck like a rag doll. I panicked — *had I killed Fire Horse?*

Blaze whinnied in concern, "What have you done, JJ?"

Fire Horse lay still for a moment. Her trainer asked if she was okay. Fire Horse came to a few moments later, but her face was covered in blood. I stood as quiet as I could in the deep water. Then Fire Horse spoke — *I hadn't killed her!* "I am okay, but I think I broke my nose and I am seeing double. I think we had better go," she calmly said to her trainer.

During the trailer ride home, I felt terrible. *What had I done?* I hadn't meant to hurt Fire Horse. Blaze also stood quietly in the trailer. We were both worried that she was badly hurt. In the trailer, Blaze nickered to me, " I know you didn't mean to hurt Fire Horse, JJ. She will be okay. I just know that she will be fine." I couldn't even respond. I was grief stricken. It was evening when we were unloaded into the pasture. I didn't see her. I was anxious. I stood alone that night. I had hurt Fire Horse. I thought she was definitely going to sell me now.

Several days passed, and I hadn't seen Fire Horse. I had quietly settled back into my routine in the herd. Blaze tried to cheer me up, but he too was concerned by the absence of Fire Horse. He came to me one afternoon and said, "JJ, I miss her too. But I know she will be back. She won't love you any less. Although, you may find yourself being ridden by the trainers again."

My life wasn't the same without her presence. I just wished I knew what was going on with her. I tried to find her in my mind, but I could not reach her. Then one afternoon I saw her. She had a white cast of some sort on her face — but I knew it was her. I galloped across the field and greeted her at the gate. Blaze trotted behind me; he too was anxious to see Fire Horse. I was so happy to see her. Other than being very cautious with me, she seemed equally happy to see me and Blaze. I sensed her calmness and her relief to see me again. She brought us carrots. Then she brought us down to the barn and groomed the both of us. I was relieved — it seemed she wouldn't sell me after all.

As Blaze had predicted, Fire Horse didn't ride me for some time. I was yet again relinquished to the trainers while she healed. When Fire Horse finally rode me again, she put me in some strange martingale system that did not allow my head to come up, and she was always under the discerning eye of the trainers. I was certain that it was one of the trainers who had put this idea into her head. They had started giving her advice about what to do with me—and the various constraints that she could use on me. These trainers always had some trick up their sleeves, but I always figured them out fairly quickly! I was a smart one! I knew that Fire Horse was extremely nervous on my back. I could understand why—I had bucked her off in my exuberance on numerous occasions, and now I had accidentally busted her face. *Would she ever trust me again?*

Fire Horse had put me back into training with the trainers while she was recovering, but I found myself insolent, and I refused to work for them. I became very difficult to catch in the pasture. At this point, her trainers refused to work with me. They told Fire Horse I was dangerous and stubborn, and that she should sell me or have me put down. Fire Horse was devastated. In her desperation, she started to look for alternative solutions. Then someone told her that she should take me to a cowboy who could "fix me."

A VISIT TO THE COWBOY

It was an early summer morning. I was munching on my hay quietly next to Blaze as the sun rose in the distance. I was surprised to see Fire Horse so early. She told me we were both going to spend some time working with a cowboy who would help us work through our problem. She was convinced that the throwing of my head was a behavioral problem. I am not sure that is how I would have classified it. It was a habit that I had picked up long ago on the racetrack—it had been especially useful in relieving tension when I was placed on the hot walker for hours on end. Now it seemed that I used my head as a weapon when I got agitated or nervous. This is how I accidentally broke Fire Horse's face, and probably how

I had come close to taking off a number of the trainers' noses as well. I really didn't mean to do it; it was just something that seemed to happen when I got frustrated or nervous.

She loaded me into the trailer. I whinnied, "Bye Blaze. I'll see you in a few hours." But I didn't see Blaze in a few hours—it was months. Fire Horse had enrolled us in an apprenticeship program together. It seemed that we were both going to be educated together over the course of the summer. I wasn't sure about this, but I knew that as long as she was in this with me, then everything would be okay.

Over the course of the summer months, Fire Horse and I spent many hours working with the cowboy. He showed her how to use the round pen to control my speed and direction. In the early days, I would spend hours each day working in the round pen and as time went by, things seemed to get easier for everyone. I was more relaxed, and Fire Horse was more skilled in working with me. The cowboy showed her how to get me accustomed to "spooky objects." At first I didn't like these games, and they truly scared me. A big blue tarp, a bright yellow rain slicker, and a bag of noisy cans chased me. Once I got the hang of this game, though, we had fun. These "spooky objects" didn't bother me anymore. I was tied to trees when I wasn't working so that I could get used to spending time with myself. I didn't like this in the beginning either. But as time went on, I grew to enjoy my "quiet time" in the shady spots. Fire Horse started working on improving my flexibility and balance from the ground. I must admit that my body was feeling much better than it had in a long time, and I enjoyed my days with Fire Horse. When she wasn't working with me, she would work other young horses around the property. I enjoyed just watching the various activities around the ranch.

At the end of the summer, on our last day at the ranch, Fire Horse and I were photographed doing a variety of our exercises in the round pen. I liked hearing the comments from the photographer about how beautiful I was. I hadn't heard those words since I was a young colt. When I peeked over Fire Horse's shoulder and caught a glimpse of some of the captured photos in the camera, I was amazed at what I saw. My coat glistened again and my ribs were no longer exposed. *I was a handsome guy!* I learned that our photos would be used in a book that the cowboy was writing on how to build a dream horse. *Maybe I would be famous after all!*

A HUNTING EXPEDITION

After my summer adventure with the cowboy, I returned back to my pasture with Blaze. Blaze greeted me with a nicker when he saw the trailer pull up to the pasture. I whinnied back. I was excited to be back home. After we played and frolicked for a bit, I told him all about my summer. Blaze told me how much I had changed since he had last seen me and he nickered, "JJ, you have a sparkle in your eye that I haven't seen before. You look healthy!" I found myself as the head of the pasture with my regained strength and confidence. Over the next few weeks, Fire Horse and I continued to play with all the exercises we had learned while working with the cowboy.

We went on leisurely rides and I was not placed back into any training programs. I felt so relieved — *life was good again.*

Shortly after our return from our summer adventure with the cowboy, an event changed the course of my life. It was a cool autumn night. Blaze and I were munching quietly on our evening hay under the light of the full moon. My senses were awakened when I heard a strange vehicle drive up the outer road leading through an apple orchard that abutted our pasture. My body awakened — for something did not feel right. There was loud and boisterous laughter coming from the car. I was immediately alerted by this strange noise. We never had visitors late at night, and something didn't feel right about this situation. The car drove slowly by the pasture. I saw no one get out, but the adrenaline surged through my body. All of a sudden I heard a loud "bang." *Ouch!* Something had hit me on my haunches. In that instant, I realized that someone was shooting at me! I whinnied loudly to anyone who might hear me, "Help!" I galloped as fast I could. It seemed that my life depended on it. My lungs began to ache as I tried to gallop away from the aggressors shooting at me. I thought my racehorse training was coming in quite handy at that moment. The faster I ran, the more laughter and shouts came from the car. In my desperation to run away from any impending shots, my foot landed in a hole, and I found myself flipped over on the ground. I lay still on the ground for a moment. I wasn't sure what had happened, but I found it difficult to get up. My lack of movement must have scared this group, as they quickly drove off. Blaze trotted over to me. Somehow I had become the target, and they had not shot at him.

"Are you okay?" he asked me anxiously. "Those crazy people were shooting at you with BB guns, " he added.

I replied weakly, "Blaze, I think something is not right. I landed on my back when I flipped over. I am in extreme pain."

Blaze nudged me up, and he stood with me through the night. I was quite scared and afraid to move. With optimism, he whispered to me, "Let's wait for Fire Horse. She'll know what to do. She'll take care of you. I know she will."

I waited for what seemed like an eternity. Fortunately, Fire Horse arrived early the next morning, completely unaware of what had happened. When she came into the pasture, she sensed immediately that something was wrong with me. She ran her hands over me. When she reached the end of my back, I buckled to my knees in pain. She immediately gave me something for the pain, and then loaded me into the trailer. It seemed as though we drove for hours. When we arrived, a veterinary team met us. I was palpated, probed, injected, and scanned. I had multiple x-rays and ultrasound scans. I was numb to the pain, but I was still very aware that something was quite wrong.

My fears were realized when I saw Fire Horse. Her eyes were filled with tears. The veterinarian had told her that she should consider putting me down. The prognosis was not good. Fire Horse asked if I could be injected for pain management. She told the veterinarians that she wanted another expert opinion before she made any decisions. We journeyed back to my pasture. I was to be injected and given oral medication daily to manage my pain.

The next day Fire Horse arrived with her "second expert." I recognized him immediately. It was the chiropractor—the same horse doctor who had helped Blaze. I immediately felt reassured by his presence. He was more optimistic, but he told Fire Horse that I had likely fractured my spinal process. He discussed with her my long-term prognosis. I overheard him say that my only chance was to be given time to heal, but that it would be a critical combination of light work and rest, and absolutely no riding until I was fully recovered. He suggested turning me out on hilly terrain, and he told her it would probably take a year at a minimum for me to heal. Fire Horse responded quite optimistically, "I think I have the perfect place where I can take JJ to recover." I was still quite nervous. *Would I ever be sound again?* I made the retirees look spry as I attempted to slowly walk around the pasture. Blaze assured me, "It will be okay, JJ. This doctor helped me. If he told Fire Horse that you will recover, then I know that you will. Just trust that it will all work out." I nodded with some sense of reassurance. Blaze was a kind and comforting spirit. He reminded me of my old friend Remy. I trusted that Fire Horse would do everything in her power to help me, and in my heart I knew I would recover.

JJ AND BLAZE MOVE TO THE MOUNTAIN

Shortly after my prognosis, Fire Horse loaded both Blaze and me into her trailer. She told us that we would be going home to live with her on her mountain ranch. We had a long journey ahead—but she assured us it would be wonderful to all live together.

We drove up the mountain slowly in her trailer. There seemed to be an endless number of mountain switchbacks. Fire Horse had opened our windows fully on this backcountry road. I couldn't resist hanging my head out to soak in the view. But poor Blaze was trailer sick. The switchbacks were making the poor guy feel terrible, and he looked to be the same color as his alfalfa hay.

"Hey Blaze, try sticking your head out and get some of this fresh mountain air. I think it will make you feel better," I offered. He tried this for a while but then he waited for the long journey to end in silence.

When we finally arrived at her ranch, Fire Horse unloaded us both. I don't think Blaze had ever been so happy to be out of a trailer. Fire Horse let us graze for a few moments. She told us we were home. Her house was simple and overlooked our large pasture. There was an open-air style barn that she told us her family had helped her build. She also had a large enclosed sand arena. She turned us out in the sand arena, and we rolled in the luxurious softness of the sand. Actually, Blaze rolled and I attempted to roll very gingerly. She then turned us out into an enormous pasture. Her ranch was beautiful. It was located on a mountain, and the terrain on the property was rolling hills with numerous oak trees and two ponds. Blaze and I were free to roam over most of the property. *This was horse heaven.*

On our first day on the ranch, we spent hours exploring our new home. We had wonderful fun exploring our surroundings. In the early evening, Fire Horse collected us from the pasture, put warm blankets on each of us, and then put us in deeply bedded open stalls. We each had shelter, but we also had a paddock that we could share together. We had fresh water and grain. I hadn't had such luxury since my days on the racetrack. This was better, though—I could see

Fire Horse's house from my stall and from anywhere in the pasture. I felt safe here. It felt like home.

Our first night on the ranch, we were greeted by a pack of coyotes moving through the range. I was anxious. I thought they might eat us; I had never lived in the wild before. But Blaze was calm as always. His earlier life had made him quite comfortable living in the wilderness. He assured me that we were fine. Fire Horse came over and also checked on us—we were safe! The next morning, before the sun was up, Fire Horse arrived. She turned us out in our large pasture, fed us our morning hay, and took off our blankets. She gave us each a big pat and told us she loved us. She was going off to work and asked that we not get into trouble.

Fire Horse worked a lot of hours. She told us that she was a professor. Some days we only saw her early in the morning and late in the evening. But other days she worked from home, and those were the days that I liked best. She would often walk out on to her deck just to check on us. Or she would just come over and visit with us. I really liked having her around. She provided me with great sense of reassurance, and I always felt at home in her presence. When she was traveling or unable to be around, she had a kind, elderly neighbor who would take care of us. He was a kind man, and both Blaze and I felt very comfortable knowing he was looking after us.

Blaze and I enjoyed our time on the ranch. The rolling hills were strengthening my back, and each day I felt a little better. Over several months, I started to feel like my old self again. I began to express my exuberance with my renewed health, and Blaze and I would often trot and canter around the property for fun.

As my athleticism returned, Fire Horse began to work with me in her round pen. Then she would take me for long walks. She started a regimen of ground driving with me so that I could regain my strength. She would put me in long lines and I would get to walk or trot ahead of her. We would often take long walks in our long lines and visit the neighboring ranches.

When my back was no longer sore, Fire Horse began taking me out for long trail rides on her ranch and the neighboring properties. I grew strong from this work, and my body felt great. One day Fire Horse had taken Blaze out of the pasture first and left me behind. "Where are you going?" I whinnied. I am not sure whether I was more worried that she was taking Blaze or that she hadn't taken me first. Immediately I felt a sense of abandonment—and then panic. *I had to find them.* I jumped the five-foot fence that separated me from Blaze and Fire Horse. Actually, I hadn't thought much about the fence—it was merely an obstacle in my path, and I certainly knew that I was capable of clearing such a height. I trotted up behind them, and I startled Fire Horse.

"JJ Luck! " she exclaimed, "How did you get out?" She put us both in our stalls. Then she went to see if she had accidentally left the gate to the pasture open. When she returned, she said, "JJ, I think it is time to go back to work." I thought for a moment. *Weren't we already working?* But then she added her inquiry to me, " What do you think? Do you think we should try going back to three-day eventing? You are an exceptional jumping horse. That is, after all, why I bought you!"

I had mixed feelings about this query. I loved to jump. I loved to gallop. I loved to be out with Fire Horse. However,

I did not like being packaged up into some tight ball with various constraining devices — and I did not like trainers! Fire Horse assured me that we would still live at home but that we would trailer down for lessons and events. She assured me that things would be different this time and that she would find a trainer whom we both liked. I was still somewhat hesitant, but I was willing to go along with her plan.

THREE-DAY EVENTING

Our first few outings back down the mountain were fun.
Fire Horse had found a trainer who specialized in three-day
eventing and this trainer was eager to work with us. Fire Horse
trailered us down the mountain for my jumping lessons and
then we would come back to the ranch. She would always
bring Blaze along for company. I thought poor Blaze wouldn't

like going up and down that mountain road very often, but he was always a good sport about it.

One weekend we went off for cross-country "schooling," and we got to jump lots of cross-country jumps — logs, ditches, banks, and water courses. I was so excited I found myself bucking after the jumps. Fortunately, Fire Horse stayed on and we had no mishaps. At the end of our schooling weekend, the trainer told Fire Horse that she thought I was bored jumping the smaller jumps and that it might be better for me if I was schooling over the larger and more challenging jumps. She encouraged Fire Horse to let her assistant trainer ride me over the larger courses.

I saw the look on Fire Horse's face. I knew she was heartbroken again. She wanted what was best for me, and she thought that would be having someone else ride me so that I could realize my jumping potential. I wished I could explain to her that I just wanted her to ride me. So what if it took a little longer to get to the bigger jumps? But that was not meant to be. Fire Horse relinquished me into the hands of the trainer again. This time, however, I was still able to live at home with Fire Horse. We would trailer down twice a week for training rides, and then Fire Horse would work with me back at the ranch. We took lots of long rides into the wilderness surrounding her ranch and often we would pony Blaze along with us.

My first event was held in winter, a few months before the regular competition season kicked off. We arrived on the fair grounds late in the evening. Fire Horse settled Blaze and me into our stalls and provided us with plenty of fresh hay and water. All was quiet on the grounds except for the sound of many munching horses surrounding us. Blaze seemed quite peaceful, and his calm presence was also reassuring for me. We both slept soundly that night. In the morning, Fire Horse arrived early with our grain and more hay. While I ate my breakfast, she groomed me and braided my mane into tight little buttons. I never really understood why horses had to have their manes braided. Fire Horse assured me it was so that I would look extra handsome when I was in the dressage court with the judge. When I had finished my breakfast, Fire Horse took me for a long walk so that I could stretch my legs. The air was literally electric. There were power lines overhead, and there was also a train that ran adjacent to the cross-country course. This external stimulus had made me quite excited. Fire Horse found a large, abandoned area near the dressage courts. She lunged me on a long line so that I could release some of my pent-up energy. It felt good to move, and it was a great relief to trot and canter a bit. When we returned to the stall, Fire Horse tacked me up. I noticed my saddle and bridle were unusually clean. Fire Horse must have been busy. She also had a bright white pad that she placed under the saddle. She told me I looked stunning. She then handed me over to the trainer who was riding me in the show. I know that Fire Horse wished she were the one showing me. I wished the same. My rider and I headed off for the warm-up ring. Today was the first day of the event. We would be tested on our dressage. The judges would be evaluating us on how well we moved. They would judge the quality of our walk, trot, and canter, as well as the quality of the transitions between the gaits. We were to ride a specific test and ride the required geometric pattern set forth in that standardized test. In the warm-up ring, I could feel the energy of the competition. This energy made me quite tense, and I couldn't relax. Fire Horse looked over at me with some concern. I was ridden for a long time by the assistant trainer until I settled down. About that time, our number was called and we rode over to the dressage arena. We trotted around the outside of the arena. The dressage court was adorned with large letters that were placed along the sides of the arena in what seemed to be very specific locations. The letters were painted black on large white blocks. Atop each block was pot of flowers. I had never seen such a spectacle, and I shied away from these adorned large letter blocks. To add to my distress, we had to ride by the judge's booth at one end of the arena. Just as we passed her booth, she rang a bell to let us know that we could enter the arena. I nearly jumped out of my skin. It brought back sudden memories of the starting bell on race days. We trotted into the arena. I was tense. We were heading straight for the judge with the scary bell. I was nervous, and my head was up in full alert. I felt the added pressure of the rein against my bit. I think I was supposed to have my head down and be "accepting of the bit," but in that moment I couldn't be accepting of anything. Strange horses were cantering in the adjacent arena. I could feel the vibration of the train as it passed the field across the way. I was ready to explode. I did my best to do what was asked of me in this test, but I know that my rider was not pleased. I felt her tension mount as the test progressed. I had no idea what this looked like to the judge, but I knew that things were not going well by the look on Fire Horse's face. She looked deeply concerned, and the trainer standing next to her did not look pleased either. When we left the arena, the trainer said, "Clearly we need to work on JJ's dressage." *I had heard that comment one too many times in my life.*

Fire Horse took me back to the stall where she untacked me and took out my button braids. What a relief. She gave me a big pat, and said that tomorrow would be a better day. She told me I would be jumping for the next two phases and that was something I very much enjoyed. She gave me some more hay and took Blaze for a long walk.

The next day arrived quickly. Fire Horse had arrived early with our breakfast. This was cross-country day, so she did not have to braid me. She tacked me up and warmed me up on a long line again. Then, as she had done the day before, she relinquished me to my rider and we headed off to the warm-up arena. The arena was filled with a number of jumps. There were all sorts of horses going every which way. While this bothered me in the dressage court, it had little effect on my ability to focus on jumping. All I needed was to be pointed in the general direction of a jump and I knew my job. Once we were warmed up, we headed out to the cross-country field. There were all sorts of obstacles. From my vantage point, I observed bank jumps, ditches, logs, and a water course. Each jump had a numbered flag by its side. We waited in a starting box until our buzzer went off. This was reminiscent of the starting gate at the racetrack but much more benign. When I heard the buzzer, I felt a little whip on my behind. I gave a little buck in protest—*no whip was necessary for me.* I would have no trouble keeping minimum speed on this course. We approached our first jump— it was a fallen log, and I easily cleared it. Then there was a hay bale jump, followed by a ditch, and a small drop off from a bank. Next we galloped through the water course and then all the remaining jumps just came so quickly and easily. I was thoroughly enjoying myself. This was fun. I only wished that Fire Horse were on my back. It seemed like we had hardly started and then we were crossing the finish line. Fire Horse was there to greet me. She had a big smile on her face, as did the trainer. "Clearly, jumping is JJ's venue," she said to Fire Horse. Fire Horse smiled, and I think I smiled back to her.

The third day of the event was the show jumping phase. Again I needed to be braided, but Fire Horse was kind enough to do this while I ate my morning hay. Somehow the distraction of breakfast made this process easier for both of us. Much like the previous day, this was an easy and enjoyable day for me. I was warmed up in the same jumping arena. Then we went over to the stadium-jumping arena for our last phase of the competition. We entered the arena and cantered around in a circle enclosing a number of the jumps. There were many jumps of various types, and they were painted in bright colors and decorated with various potted flowers. Somehow the same flowers that had startled me on dressage day did not bother me in my stadium jumping. We cantered the first vertical with ease, and I realized that these would be easy jumps for me to clear. There were several combinations and a spread jump known as an oxer. I made little work of these obstacles and easily cleared the course. As I left the arena, many smiling faces welcomed me. At the end of the competition, I overheard the trainer say to Fire Horse that she was quite pleased with my first show and that she had a number of shows in mind for me that coming spring.

When the eventing season resumed in spring, we had a full schedule. We would pack up on a Thursday night and get to the show grounds late at night. Fire Horse, true to her word, always brought Blaze with us. I don't think the trainer liked that she did this, nor did she like that Fire Horse kept me up on her ranch rather than in the trainer's barn. But it was the only way that Fire Horse could live with the situation — and it seemed reasonable to me. I always did quite well on the cross-country and show-jumping phases, but I never did very well in dressage. The moment I entered the dressage court I would find my head up in the air as I became a bit anxious about being "collected." After several such incidents of poor dressage scores, my training began to include lunging in various constraints to "collect me." I didn't like this — and I knew that Fire Horse also had reservations about this too. Over the next few events, my dressage score improved, but my body was starting to feel sore again. Over the next few months, I actually placed in a few events. That is, I won a ribbon. Fire Horse was always there to take my photograph. She was like a proud parent. However, we both wished that we could be earning those ribbons together.

The culmination of my eventing career occurred at a big three-day event. It had required a ten-hour trailer ride, and I found myself a bit tired by the time we arrived. Poor Blaze was exhausted from the trip. The show grounds were adjacent to a racetrack, and I was exhilarated the moment we arrived. When I was settled into my stall and munching on my hay, I looked around for Blaze. He was nowhere in sight. I whinnied, "Blaze, where are you?" But there was no response. I paced in my stall and was very anxious about his whereabouts. Blaze always came to my events. He would cheerfully call to me each time he saw me from his stall. But this time the trainer had him placed across the road so that I would not be distracted by his presence. Yet it had the opposite effect on me. This also upset Fire Horse, as she had requested side-by-side stalls for us. Fire Horse looked tired. She would work Blaze across the street, and then she would groom me and do ground work with me to get me ready for my show. Because Fire Horse wasn't the person showing me, she was not allowed to be on my back while we were on the show grounds. This disheartened both of us.

My training on the day before the big event started was intense. It seemed like we schooled for hours on my dressage. Unfortunately, in this process, I became sore in my back. Fire Horse asked the trainer if she should withdraw me from the competition, but her trainer told her to give me a small amount of Bute and see how I looked in the morning. I knew Fire Horse was worried about me when she checked on me that night. "I am sorry, JJ. I don't want you to be sore. I hope I am doing the right thing for you," she said to me as she massaged my sore back. By the time she left, I was falling to sleep, and I slept soundly that night.

The next morning I was still a bit sore, but Fire Horse took me for a long walk and did various exercises with me to get me flexible. I actually felt pretty good by the time she was through. But when we got to the warm-up ring and my rider was on my back, I found myself tense and tight again. I did the best that I could in the dressage arena, but it probably wasn't the greatest score. The next two days I basked in the cross-country and show jumping phases. I would have flourished in two-day eventing—with no dressage! *Couldn't someone create such a sport?* At the end of the weekend, I had placed reasonably well, but my body was very sore. The trainer told Fire Horse that there were a number of bigger shows that I should go to that summer and that I should move up to the next level. She then told Fire Horse that I would need much more training to improve my dressage scores and she suggested that maybe I needed another trip back to the cowboy to "fix" my "high headedness." My mind raced as I heard this comment. *Why do I need to be "fixed"? I am perfect just as I am. Why do I have to do this impractical dressage stuff? Maybe I should just be a jumping horse.*

Fire Horse trailered us home that night. It was very late by the time we got home, and we were so tired by the time that we got home that Blaze and I each collapsed into our beds of straw. The next morning Fire Horse came to check on us, and she looked as tired as I felt. She told me she was very proud of me and she was very sorry that I had gotten so sore. Fire Horse whispered in my ear, "Maybe this three-day eventing isn't our path, JJ. I don't want to hurt you, and I don't want to lose you into this silly, competitive world." Then she patted me and said, "Let's take a few weeks off and see what happens."

NATURAL HORSEMANSHIP

After a few weeks of rest and relaxing rides around the ranch, Fire Horse announced her plan to me. "JJ, I have decided that we are going to take a break from eventing this summer. Instead, we are going to go off to a natural horsemanship clinic for the summer. Blaze will come with us. It will be fun. You'll see!" One thing was certain—life with Fire Horse was never dull.

We packed up all of our tack and loaded up the trailer. We were off for another adventure. When we arrived at this new ranch, I discovered that there were many horses and owners that were also here for the clinic. We would be working with a master horseman who would be teaching our owners about natural horsemanship. The first day of the clinic all of the horses were turned out together. We definitely had a pecking order that needed to be sorted out. There were some horses from another part of the country that definitely ruled their territory of the arena. I decided to stay in the "neutral territory" and away from them when possible. I met two friends in the herd—Tristan and Juan. I found myself hanging out with them, as they seemed like good companions in this strange environment. Tristan is an older Thoroughbred who looked like he could be my older brother—except that he has white socks and a blaze down his nose. I am pure chestnut. Juan is an Andalusian cross who looked like a fancy Spanish horse with a long flowing black mane over his steel gray body. We had a few hours of leisure time each day and we would play, roll, and sunbathe together.

At the start of the summer there were at least twenty horses and their respective owners in the clinic. This made for great fun for the horses as we would spend hours turned out each day as a herd. In the first few days of the clinic, it became clear that we were all here for some specific reason. Fire Horse and I had come so that she could overcome her fear of jumping with me and to learn how to deal with my "high headedness." I heard various owners talk of the difficulties with their horses—he bucks me off, he rears, she won't tie, she won't trailer load, he bites, he won't go forward, he spooks on the trail, etc. The list went on and on. It would take a while for everyone to realize that these were not horse problems but rather people problems. Most of our habits and phobias had been man-made, and the only way to "fix us" was to also "fix our human." This was a humbling experience for those who thought they would bring their horses to a cowboy and have us "fixed."

Over the first few weeks of the clinic, our owners learned to work with us using cowboy halters (a cowboy halter is a rope halter that is attached to a twelve-foot lead rope, and there are no breakable parts). They learned to lead us and to walk with us. They learned about having a safety bubble. This was refreshing to us. Horses are herd animals, and we rely on body language for communication—it was nice that our owners were finally learning our language. As our owners became more adept about clearly communicating to us, all of our respective relationships began to improve. Our owners learned to move our haunches and shoulders. They learned to ride us in just a halter—so that they learned to use their seat and legs before they used their hands. This was such a relief from my prior dressage training where so much emphasis had been placed on control of my head by use of strong bits, reins, and restraints. Fire Horse was finally learning that true collection came from behind and not from the front. That is, I could be "collected" with leg and seat into a soft hand. This was far more comfortable for me, and I learned to use my body to be in self-carriage.

Our owners learned to escalate aids so that as they became clearer about their intentions with their body language, it became much more fluid for us to work together. This was a great relief to all of us. As the horses, we had always been blamed for the problems. Now our owners were making changes in themselves. Here at "horse camp" our owners learned that the horse is perfect just as he is—and that if they wanted a better relationship with their horse, then they had to learn our language—and if they wanted a better horse, they had to become better horse communicators. Several of the owners didn't take to well to this philosophy and dropped out. Fire Horse and I stayed.

Over the next several weeks, the horsemanship clinic picked up in intensity. We would spend up to eight hours a day working together. We would work in the halter, in the round pen at liberty, and in the arena as a herd. When we worked in the halter, our owners learned to lead us from a twelve-foot distance. Our owners learned to change our directions and send us around obstacles, and then this progressed to liberty work. The liberty work was done without any halters or bridles—in this work, the horses were at liberty and we thoroughly enjoyed that freedom. Each day our owners worked with us on the ground and in the saddle. We were exposed to all sorts of crazy things. We learned to stand quiet while the sounds of a bullwhip or sirens were going off. This was introduced to us as a herd. The first time I heard the bull whip, it was deafening in my ears. I nearly jumped out of my skin. Some of the horses were not bothered by this loud noise. Fire Horse would place me among the calmest horses, and she would stroke my neck until I relaxed. Eventually, it was just a noise, and I learned to just listen to the energy of Fire Horse. If she wasn't concerned, there was no reason for me to be. I grew to trust her deeply in this work. One day we had a real live fire engine come into the arena—with flares and smoke!! Again, I just followed the relaxed horses and became reassured by the calming presence and confidence of Fire Horse. Some days we had full-out obstacle courses in the arena. We went over bridges and through tarps. We walked and trotted past flares.

We even pushed an enormous red ball around the arena—
and sometimes we would get to play horse soccer with the
ball too! I began to enjoy the various challenges that faced us
each day. The greatest benefit of this work was that I found
myself growing calmer and more reassured about my life and
myself in general.

The day of ultimate trust came on the day that our owners
learned how to gently lay us down. Lying down is the most
vulnerable position for a horse, because in order to lie down,
he must surrender all of his feet. As horses, we tend only to
lay down in our stalls or when we are surrounded by the
safety of a herd. A lone horse lying down in the wild is likely
to become someone's lunch. We are prey animals, and we
were all instinctively aware of that. The first day that we were
laid down, many of the horses were terrified and fought with
all their might at doing this. The horseman gently used a rope
around a front leg and the cowboy halter was used to gingerly
guide us down. As we began to drop to our knees, all pressure
was released, and we soon learned that we were not going to
be thrown down but rather guided down softly. Over time we
could each do this with a light touch, knowing that we would
be safe when we were lying by the side of our owner. As my
confidence grew, I offered my feet readily to Fire Horse, for I
knew she would never hurt me.

I was always glad I had Fire Horse and my friends Tristan
and Juan with me in the clinic. We would often try to stick
together in chaotic moments. I often tried to stay behind
Tristan, as he seemed to be wise to this strange world. He
too had an insightful owner named Spirit Horse. He had
been with her since he was a youngster. Tristan told me they

had been doing this natural horsemanship stuff for nearly a decade. "Do you like this work?" I asked him one day. Tristan nickered to me, "I really like it. Especially playing with the big red ball!" I nodded in agreement, and I shared, "This sure beats my old training, and I like hanging out with Fire Horse and my horse friends." In the evenings, I would see Blaze, and I would tell him of my great daily adventures. He had the luxury of the day out in a paddock, and then Fire Horse would work with him in the evenings after he had his dinner. I wondered if she ever slept!

As the clinic came to a close, we spent the last few weeks working at liberty. That is, the horses were worked without any halters or constraints. There were only about seven horses (and owners) left and we would work in the arena together each day under the tutelage of the master horseman. We would come into the arena in the morning, and sometimes we would get a chance to run together as a herd, and our owners would control our direction and patterns. We would be groomed and saddled by our owner, and if one of us wandered away, we were put to work and then sent back to our owners. Over time we realized the best place to be was with our human. *I already knew that!* We followed our owners anywhere they went. Fire Horse liked to play a game of tag with me. She would run a slalom pattern through cones and around the arena. I loved to canter closely behind her. Everyone was always in awe as they saw us play this game together. I am sure it looked like I might run her down at any moment, but I would never hurt Fire Horse. We learned to canter around our owners in a tight circle, and we learned to leg yield (move sideways) away from and toward them with out any constraints. The best part was learning to jump large obstacles at liberty. There would be a whole range of jumps and obstacles set up around the arena. We were to jump each one as we came to it. Our people were on the ground with us. After we jumped our obstacle, we would turn around and return to our human partner. Sometimes I got ahead of myself—I would jump the obstacle and then another, and then I would return to Fire Horse. This was my favorite game. I could out-jump any other horse in the arena. We would build jump-off courses, and I always won. *I loved this liberty work!*

As our groundwork improved, we moved this liberty work into the saddle. With the instruction of the horseman, our owners were taught to use two sticks or a small loop around our neck instead of a bridle. The first day that we did this, Fire Horse was petrified. I liked to lead the herd, and after all, I was a retired race horse, and she often found herself galloping while everyone was else was still cantering and struggling to keep up. I would often recruit Tristan to join me at the front of the pack. I don't think Fire Horse or Spirit Horse were too fond of this situation either. Eventually I was relinquished to being ridden by the master horseman. He wanted to demonstrate that my speed could be regulated without the use of a bit or reins. He rode me around the arena, and he used his legs and seat to regulate my speed. He was much stronger than Fire Horse. I protested at first. *I'll show you a thing or two!* I slung my head backward and then I offered several of my world-class bucks, figuring I could launch him. We were having a private rodeo—but he didn't leave my back. Instead, he just made me work harder. I tried to throw my head in defense, but then he put his spurs into my side until I began to lower my head and soften. As I yielded, he released all pressure and gave me a pat on the neck. He repeated the process until I was a relaxed horse. He then got off and handed me back to Fire Horse. I was drenched and exhausted. I had never lost a battle before. Fire Horse was clearly frightened. The horseman jokingly told her I would make a good bucking horse! He then worked with Fire Horse and me until we were able to go around the arena calmly—and more importantly, he worked with her on my "high headedness." Every time I would put my head up in resistance, she would apply pressure with both of her legs. When I dropped my head, she took all pressure off and gave me a pat. Together we learned that I didn't need to throw my head anymore, and we began to trust each other completely. Soon I found myself leading the herd work—not because I galloped to the front, but because I could regulate the herd. We would walk, trot, or canter in any pattern and in any pace that Fire Horse chose.

Our last phase of liberty work involved jumping without a bridle. Fire Horse and I had worked through my high-headedness issue, but now Fire Horse had to face her biggest fear—jumping me—and this time without a bridle. I could feel her tension mounting. Everyone offered her support. Spirit Horse said, "Fire Horse, you can do this—just remember to breathe." As we cantered to the first set of barrels (they were only about three feet high—an easy feat for me), I prepared to jump, but something didn't feel right. Fire Horse panicked and didn't follow my motion. I cleared the jump, but she didn't—she had been left behind and had fallen off my side. She didn't move. I was horrified that she might be hurt again.

She got up, but she could barely walk. I was heartbroken—*how could this have happened?*

That night I didn't see Fire Horse. I paced in my stall all night. Blaze tried to reassure me, "Fire Horse is tough—she'll be all right." The next day I saw her, but she was on crutches. She had pinched a nerve in her leg and was bruised, but she would be okay. Fire Horse assured me, "JJ, you were a good boy. I just panicked. I trust you! Give me a day or two of rest and then I'll be good as new, and we'll conquer those jumps!" As always, she was true to her word with me. In a few days time, she saddled me up without my bridle and we jumped our first set of barrels. All of her friends in the clinic encouraged her. Once we cleared that first jump together, we were free of our fears—we could jump anything. Over the next few weeks, we found ourselves jumping the same obstacles that we had cleared easily on the ground. *We were unstoppable now!*

The culmination of the summer clinic was a public demonstration. Hundreds of people were invited to watch this special event. We were bathed and groomed to look our best. For once I didn't mind. I was going to make Fire Horse proud, and I was going to make her look good! There were initial demonstrations, including a vaulting team. Then it was our time. We came out in front of this large audience, and we each took a spot in the arena. Fire Horse had transformed. She had come to this clinic with fears. Over the past several months, she had bought me a beautiful western saddle and bridle. She too had changed her attire—she now sported cowboy boots, chaps, a western shirt, and a great cowgirl hat. *Now she looked like Fire Horse!* We looked great together. I cantered around her with pride.

All of us had transformed. Juan looked magical as his long mane flowed in his liberty work, and Tristan looked pleased as he cantered around Spirit Horse. Even the territorial horses, Junior, Riley, Charlie, Chance, and Grey, who belonged to the world's greatest cowboy and his family, had become my friends. We looked fabulous out there in the arena. People were in awe as they saw us jump large obstacles at liberty and then turn around after each one and return to our owners. Fire Horse and I were the highlight as I easily cleared the largest jumps. We then set up an obstacle course that included a bridge, tarps, and flares. The fire engine was in place, and its alarms blared. We played with the large, red ball. The audience watched in amazement as we calmly navigated all of these challenges. Then we were laid down in front of the audience. As the day wound down, the audience was treated to flying lead changes and a herd ride at liberty, and finally the jump–off.

Fire Horse and I were unstoppable, and we cleared each jump with ease! The crowd cheered! I was glowing with pride. However, we had one mishap at the end of the day. The crowd had cheered for Spirit Horse to jump Tristan bridleless too. Spirit Horse and Tristan had not planned to jump in the demonstration, but with the encouragement of the crowd, they agreed to take the jumps at liberty. They cleared the first jump, and the crowd roared. Then Tristan balked at the next jump and at the last minute he jumped, but Spirit Horse didn't make it. She hit the ground hard. The audience was silent. But like Fire Horse she was determined. She got up and made light of the incident. She climbed back on and finished her ride. The crowd cheered for her and became alive with passion. I was so relieved. I didn't want Spirit Horse to be hurt. I would have to talk to Tristan about that little stunt! As we completed our event, the crowd all stood and applauded. We had put on a spectacular demonstration.

The next morning I was turned out in the arena for some playtime with my horse friends. We rolled in the soft sand, and we played together with ease. Over the next few days, many of the horses would be heading home and the horseman would be heading out on a tour where he would teach natural horsemanship around the country. But I wasn't going anywhere. I would be staying behind on this ranch with Blaze, Tristan, and Juan. *Hooray! No more eventing! No more trainers!* Fire Horse, Blaze, and I lived on the ranch for the next few months while the horseman was on road. Tristan and Juan stayed too. This was fantastic. For months we played together each day. Eventually Juan and his owner moved on to another farm, but before Juan and his owner left, Fire Horse approached his owner. Fire Horse said that she would be most interested in purchasing Juan if she were to ever consider selling him. Juan's owner told Fire Horse that she would consider that if that day ever came. We nickered our goodbyes to Juan as he headed down the road in his trailer. I had a feeling that I would see Juan again someday. For now, it was just Tristan, Blaze, and me holding down the fort, so to speak. We had great fun together. Spirit Horse and Fire Horse often worked together with us in the arena, and they would also take us out for great trail rides on the beach or in the beautiful, rolling hills along the coast. *Life was good.*

VIVA LAS VEGAS

As the autumn months came to an end, the master horseman returned back to the ranch. He would be teaching a month-long horsemanship clinic at his ranch before heading to Las Vegas for a demonstration. He had asked Spirit Horse and Fire Horse if they would like to participate in the clinic. He was impressed with their accomplishments while he had been on the road. Fire Horse was later invited to go to Vegas. She told me that we would both be going to Las Vegas with his team. The horses from the summer clinic that belonged to the world's greatest cowboy and his family would also be going. I was excited. *Another road trip!* We trained hard in the clinic as we prepared for the upcoming Vegas show. We would be putting on a natural horsemanship demonstration each day of the Grand National Rodeo. Fire Horse told me that we would be performing in a hotel that was built like a castle with an indoor arena that was normally used for an evening jousting show. I was excited to see all of this!

We headed out early one morning after packing up all the trailers and trucks filled with our various accessories — our jumps, tarps, bridges, flares, and of course the big red ball. I was disappointed to learn that Blaze and Tristan would be staying behind. We drove all day and into the evening. When we arrived, I was in awe of the sights along the Vegas strip. I had never seen so many lights in my life! We settled in at a little ranch a few miles away from the downtown lights. Fire Horse got me settled in and gave me a big hug, and then she whispered, "I'll see you in the morning. Tomorrow you get to go to the castle for our practice day." *Another grand adventure!*

The next morning arrived quickly. All the horses were packed up into their respective trailers. I would be going back and forth with Fire Horse each Day. I whinnied out the window with excitement. As we drove down the strip, I was in awe — there were palm trees and all sorts of extravagant hotels. One even had its own volcano! Fire Horse had dropped the window so that I could look out. I could see Fire Horse in her rear view window. She laughed as she saw that my eyes were the size of saucers. When the trailer stopped, we parked outside a medieval castle. I had never seen such a spectacle.

As we entered the castle, we went down a steep, dark ramp that emptied into a grooming room. All the other horses had already arrived. My summer friends that belonged to the cowboy and his family were there too—Junior, Riley, Charlie, Chance, and Grey! After we were groomed, we were all brought into the arena. We were all turned out together so we could meet the horseman's horses and colts too. I was growing very excited about this upcoming week in the castle. As I settled in, I was in awe as I took in my surroundings. The arena looked like the interior of a fort adjoined by castle walls and a drawbridge. It was surrounded by at least one thousand seats so that an audience could sit close to the action.

On our practice day, we were exposed to all the various lights and sounds that we would be exposed to during the upcoming demonstrations. There were spotlights and fascinating lighting patterns that moved all over the ground of the arena under our feet. At first I shied away from all the strange colored holes that were appearing in front of my feet. Soon I realized that these were not actual holes that I could fall into but just colored spots that were moving.

I was a bit nervous on the first day of the performance. We were backstage in the dark waiting for the program to start. I could hear "The Star-Spangled Banner" playing, and I knew that soon we would be invited into the arena to give our demonstration. I could feel Fire Horse's heart beating as fast as mine. She too was a bit nervous. When our names were called, I trotted alongside of Fire Horse as we entered the arena. We were welcomed by what seemed like thousands of cheering fans. The energy of the audience was exuberant, and it was almost overwhelming. In my nervousness, I tried to hide behind Fire Horse, but she too was also taking shelter in me. We compromised and she stood by my side and gave me a proud pat.

Each of us was introduced to the audience. When it was time to introduce me, Fire Horse did her zigzag run around the arena and through the other horses and their humans. I cantered closely behind her — hot on her heels! *There might be a dragon in that audience — I wasn't going to lose her!!* I heard on the loud speakers in the audience, "This large chestnut is a Thoroughbred-Appaloosa cross named JJ." The story of my early life with Fire Horse was told to the audience. This included reference to my earlier behavior when I used my head as a weapon. It was added, somewhat jokingly, that I could have had a career as a bucking bronco.

As the audience heard of our various struggles, they stared in amazement at us. They were in awe as we went through our liberty routines, as we jumped over obstacles without any constraints, and as we faced up graciously to flares, bull whips, tarps, and the large, red ball. We demonstrated flying lead changes without any bridles and then under dim lights and soothing music, we surrendered our feet and lay down with our owners. There were tears in the eyes of many in the audience as they were touched by such trust between equine and human.

The show ended each day with a jump-off. Fire Horse and I were always a highlight as I readily cleared all the obstacles with ease. People leaned out over their seats and snapped photographs of us as we cleared the largest barrels. I never missed a barrel — not all week! I was very proud of Fire Horse and myself. We seemed to have found our groove together.

At the end of each performance, the audience was invited into the arena. There would often be a crowd that would form around Fire Horse. Many complimented her on the relationship that she had with me and commented on how happy I looked. They asked her what had given her the courage to not give up on me. She replied proudly, "Just look at him — isn't it obvious — JJ is spectacular. I couldn't imagine my life without him!" One person asked her how much money it would take for her to sell me. I listened intently to her answer. She smiled and responded, "There is no amount of money for which I could ever sell this horse. He is invaluable to me." If horses could smile, then I was smiling too. *I loved my life with Fire Horse.*

A ROCKY MOUNTAIN ADVENTURE

When we returned back to the ranch, I excitedly told my adventurous story about my trip to Vegas to both Tristan and Blaze. They listened intently. They hoped that they too could go on such an adventure some day and that day would come. After the Vegas trip, Fire Horse took Blaze and me back to her ranch for a few weeks' holiday. Then we returned to the horseman's ranch for the next teaching clinic. We were then invited to go to a large horse exposition in Denver for another natural horsemanship demonstration with the horseman. I was excited about another escapade and even more enthused to learn that Blaze and Tristan would be joining me.

The morning we left for Denver, Fire Horse loaded the three of us into her trailer with fresh hay for us to munch on while we traveled. Blaze and I were accustomed to trailering, but Tristan was a bit nervous, and he hadn't trailered any great distances. Blaze and I assured him that all would be well and that we would have a great time on our trip. Each night we stopped in campgrounds across the Western states as we drove to Denver. We were always given a chance to stretch our legs after a day in the trailer, and then we were bedded in comfortable stalls with fresh water and hay each evening. We always felt safe knowing that Spirit Horse and Fire Horse were just outside our campground stalls.

At one of our stops, we had an extraordinary experience. As usual, we were given the chance to stretch and roll after a long day in the trailer. We were turned out in a big sand arena and we were all taking full advantage of the luxurious sand. We each rolled several times, and then we began to play and frolic. Then something shifted in the air. It became cool and the wind picked up. Suddenly we were not alone in the arena but were joined by two horse spirits who had once lived on the property. They joined us as we galloped around the arena. In that same moment, Spirit Horse came to check on us. She saw the spirits as they vanished over the horizon, but they had all disappeared by the time Fire Horse arrived. Spirit Horse shared what she had seen with Fire Horse. It was comforting to be in the presence of horse people who could be open to such possibilities.

When we arrived in Denver, we all had a feeling of amazement as we saw the size of the complex. Tristan was a bit anxious, but we assured him that we would be fine. Once we stretched our legs, we each settled into our respective stalls bedded high with straw. We all slept well after our long journey.

The next morning we explored the facility so that we could stretch our legs. Spirit horse led Tristan and Fire Horse led Blaze and me. I think all of our eyes were the size of saucers! The complex was bustling with all sorts of horses — draft horses, jumping horses, dressage horses, reining horses, carriage horses, and miniature horses too. There even were horses and riders in all sorts of costumes. *Was this a horse circus?*

When we entered the arena in the coliseum, we were consumed by its size, for it was as large as a football field with thousands of seats in the stadium. There were many horses in the arena doing various warm ups and we all absorbed our new surroundings. Tristan was a bit worried.

I nickered softly to him, "Hey, Tristan, it will be ok. We are here with our horse friends and just you wait — the audience will love us. They always do! You should have seen all my fans in Vegas!"

He was consumed by the sheer size of this venue, but I knew that everything would be all right. Our practice obstacles were set up and we practiced for our upcoming demonstrations over the next several days. We would be doing a similar routine to the one that we had done in Vegas. I was completely confident that this would be great fun!

On the day of our performance, we were all tied to a section of the stadium below the first row of seats. We were awaiting another performance to wrap up before we could enter the arena. It was a carriage horse demonstration, with many large draft horses and carriages. Tristan was quite anxious with this commotion, but I assured him all would be well. I had not seen horse-drawn carriages before but I found myself remembering my old friend Remy and the stories he had shared with me about pulling carriages. I was lulled into the dreamy state of my past when thundering hooves awakened me. A team of six black percherons were cantering around the arena and pulling their large cart proudly behind them. It was the grand finale of their performance. The tumultuous sound of hooves reminded me of my racing days. Poor Tristan was panicked and pulling back on his rope. I nickered out to him, "Tristan, it's just a show, no one will hurt us." Tristan settled down, and we waited for our own time in the limelight.

When our performance time came, we all entered the arena. I had already traveled with the rest of these horses to Vegas, so I knew it would be great fun. We all took our respective spots in the arena, and we were introduced to the expansive audience. There was a large round of applause welcoming us to Denver. It was electric, and I felt alive. I was proud to be standing next to Fire Horse, and I was happy to have my friends Tristan and Spirit Horse with us too. Fire Horse and I took our playful run, and the audience loved it. I think to the outsider it looks like magic to have a large chestnut horse cantering side by side his chestnut cowgirl. For me this was so much fun, and I sensed that Fire Horse also loved our playful time together.

We went through our various routines, and the audience applauded loudly. I looked over to check on my friend Tristan, but he was frightened by the size of the audience and the boisterous noise of their applause. There was little I could do to help him from across the arena. Tristan was afraid to go over one of the obstacles, and the audience became silent. I am sure the pressure was mounting for both Tristan and Spirit Horse, as now all eyes were on them. The horseman talked them through it, and they were able to jump the rest of the obstacles. The audience roared. We completed our performance with my favorite part—the jump-off. We cleared all sorts of combinations of barrels and obstacles. Fire Horse and I were one with each other as we soared through the air sans bridle over all the jumps. At the end, everyone stood and applauded. Fire Horse patted me with pride. *It was great to be so alive.*

Our days in Denver were a great success. Many people were in awe at the wonders of natural horsemanship. I wondered how many of these people would be willing to make the changes in themselves that were necessary to have the type of relationship that I have with Fire Horse. It was nice to know that we were setting an example for thousands. While at the expo we had also been captured on television, so maybe we were having an impact on more people than I knew. I was proud to know that somehow Fire Horse and I were setting an example for treating horses with dignity and respect.

The morning after our demonstration wrapped up, we were all packed up in the trailer to head back home. Blaze loaded first, then Tristan, and finally me. For the next few hours, we exchanged our stories from our experiences over the past few days. Tristan was beaming. He had never traveled so far or performed in front of a large audience like this. I told him I was proud of him.

As we drove into the evening, the air blowing through our windows grew cooler. The weather began to change into a wintry scene, and snow began to fall. We started to drive slower and slower. Finally, we stopped at a local fairground. When we were unloaded, we realized that everything was covered with several inches of snow and it was near whiteout conditions. We could barely see our noses as we walked toward a structure in the distance. As we got closer, we could see a large metal hut. It was unlike any barn I had ever seen. Fire Horse led us into the structure, and my head barely cleared the doorway. Inside were tiny stalls filled with mules and various ponies. They nickered their greetings to us as we entered. Fire Horse found us a warm set of stalls in the back and placed us inside. I could have climbed over my gate if I had chosen to, but I was too tired to try any funny business. Fire Horse gave us fresh water and hay. We all munched on our dinners and settled in for an easy sleep. Fire Horse and Spirit Horse slept in the trailer outside the door. As always, I rested easy knowing she was nearby.

The next morning was clear, and the remainder of our drive home was uneventful. On our journey home, we all exchanged our life stories. Blaze and I learned about how Tristan had found Spirit Horse and how their life had brought them into the world of natural horsemanship.

TRISTAN

On our journey home from Denver, Tristan shared with us the story of his life. "I was born many years ago late in March on a warm, sunny day. Like JJ, I am also an Arian horse and share many of the attributes of a horse born under the astrological sign of Aries. Like both of you, I am chestnut in color. I have always been admired for my striking white blaze down my nose and my white bobby socks on my hind legs. I think that, like JJ, I am not a horse that would have ever been suitable for a novice.

"I spent the first two years of my life in pasture at a beautiful Thoroughbred facility. Initially I was in pasture with my mother. I truly loved my mother. She too was a chestnut Thoroughbred, and I looked very much like her. Once I was weaned, I was turned out with other fillies and colts and enjoyed my time frolicking with them in the lush green pastures.

"When I was a bit older than two years old and not yet three, I was sold to a hunter-jumper trainer. My life was nearly the same, but I missed my old friends and my mother. When I was about three years old my new owner started me over small jumps. I think the goal was to turn me into a jumping horse. She saddled me and lunged me over jumps to see if I had any jumping potential. I liked jumping, and she seemed quite pleased with my abilities. I was still quite young, and so I was turned back out in pasture for another year or so. I don't believe that I was asked to do any real work until after I turned four years old.

"When my training started in earnest, my life changed. I was taken from my life in the pasture and placed in a stall. I had liked my pasture much better, but I grew accustomed to life in the stall. My training focused on jumping. Each day was always new and challenging, but I remember that I enjoyed jumping very much. One day, as I had been settling into my routine and enjoying my life as a prospective jumping horse, I was disheartened to learn that I was to be sold. As you know, this is very disconcerting to a horse. For we never know where we will go or who might buy us. We don't know what type of home we will have, and we don't have any idea of how we will be treated.

"While I was up for sale, a number of people came to see me. I felt a connection with one woman who came to try me out as a potential horse for herself — this, of course, was Spirit Horse. She rode me a couple of times a week out on trail rides. My owner and trainer did not like the idea of me being used as a trail horse, but I thought trail rides were quite enjoyable. I really liked being with Spirit Horse. She was looking for a horse to have of her own, and she had wanted an older, more experienced horse. I think she continued to look at other horses while she was riding me. Finally she decided that perhaps I was the right horse for her. One day, she decided to take me out on a long trail ride to see how I would fare as a trail horse. I had never seen so many strange and scary things in my life. On our ride together, we came across baby strollers, bicycles, people with backpacks and cameras, and lots of other horses coming and going. I had never seen such things. But I did my best for Spirit Horse, and at the end of that day she decided she would buy me. I was very happy.

"We stayed with my former trainer for a while, but then Spirit Horse went off to watch a clinic given by the horseman. She was fascinated by the natural horsemanship, and she initially took one of his courses and used one of his school horses. After her positive experience with this work, she brought me to work with the horseman. This was many years ago. At first I was enrolled in a basic clinic with Spirit Horse, but then we continued working with natural horsemanship for many years. Spirit Horse and I worked very hard and eventually we started helping the horseman with his other clinics. I became a baby sitter for many horses who would arrive and be frightened by some of the sensory work. You may remember that the first time a horse sees a six-foot diameter red ball or has to pass through tarps or over bridges, he can be quite scared. I helped provide confidence to an uncertain horse. This was an enjoyable time in my life with Spirit Horse.

"After several years, we moved to a facility that was closer to Spirit Horse's home. I really loved it there. I had a large stall and paddock at night when it was cool, but every day I was turned out to graze with other horses that lived on the ranch. I saw Spirit Horse nearly every day. This ranch was a co-op, so our owners did all the work around the ranch—they cleaned our stalls, they fed us, and they managed our daily turnout. Spirit Horse had been asked by many of the other boarders to teach natural horsemanship clinics on the weekends, so I had a chance to show off all the various things I had learned from the horseman over the years.

"Back in those days, I was the herd leader. I was the horse who would greet a new horse when he entered the herd. That is how I met Juan. It was several years ago, and he had arrived on a large semi-truck from some far-away state. He had traveled a great distance and was quite tired when he arrived. I welcomed him into our pasture, and we became great pals. We spent much time playing together when we were turned out in pasture each day. We all loved it on this beautiful ranch, and we nicknamed it "horse heaven." Unfortunately, our little slice of heaven was sold one day, and we all had to move to another facility. It was not nearly as nice as the life we had lived before, but at least I still had Spirit Horse and Juan in my life.

"One day, Juan's owner wanted to enhance her understanding of natural horsemanship. She approached Spirit Horse about this and it was decided that they would work with the horseman together and that they would take Juan and me too. We enrolled for a short clinic in the summer, and as you know, we stayed for the whole summer. This is where I met you both. From that time, I have been working closely with Spirit Horse on the various horsemanship demonstrations.

"I have really enjoyed these times with Spirit Horse and traveling with you both. I only wish that Juan could have come along with us to Denver. I hope that some day we can all live together again."

We all agreed that it would be nice to have Juan back in our lives and to live out in a grassy pasture that we could all enjoy. Maybe someday that would happen.

A CALAMITY

After things wound down after Denver, Tristan and I settled into another clinic on natural horsemanship. We were becoming very proficient at teaching new horses the ropes, so to speak. Spirit Horse and Fire Horse started having a larger role in the clinics, and we were often asked to give demonstrations to new students. It was great to finally be recognized for our accomplishments together. Fire Horse and I were a team, and nothing could take us apart.

One afternoon, as the new summer clinic kicked off, I almost lost Fire Horse in a calamity. There was an uneasy tension in the air that day. Fire Horse and Spirit Horse were off helping students with their horses while Tristan and I were tied to the barn outside the arena. I was growing anxious waiting for them to return. We were to give a demonstration to the class in the afternoon, and I was ready to get out of the hot sun and into the arena.

Finally, Fire Horse and Spirit Horse arrived with our grooming supplies. They groomed us and saddled us. I remained a bit unsettled. Something didn't feel right that day. Suddenly I heard a commotion. Then out of the corner of my eye, I saw Tristan pulling back with all his might. He couldn't break free from his tie, and in his panicked state, he then reared up. He knocked the hat off Spirit Horse, and she was now trapped between Tristan and me. He settled down briefly and then Fire Horse leaned across him to try to guide Spirit Horse toward me. I watched in horror as Tristan reared again. The movement of Fire Horse had frightened him. He pulled back and reared again. His hoof caught Fire Horse in the back of her head as he reared. I exclaimed, "Stop. You are hurting Fire Horse!" But he could not hear me as he was in a frightened state—his flight mechanism had been triggered and nothing could soothe him in that moment. Spirit Horse screamed as Fire Horse was dragged under the hooves of Tristan. He panicked more and continued to land on her each time he reared. What took mere seconds seemed like an eternity. Somehow Fire Horse got free of his hooves, and she lay on the ground beside Tristan. Fire Horse didn't move, and I saw that she was covered in blood. I was so scared that I could not move or articulate any sounds. My mind raced. *What would I do if I lost Fire Horse?* People came running to see what the commotion was all about, but no one dared touch Fire Horse for fear of causing further injury. An ambulance came and took Fire Horse away, but I did not know her destiny. I was filled with grief and anxiety.

I was taken away and put in a nearby paddock with Tristan. All of my pent-up emotion needed an outlet. It was as though I couldn't control myself, and I attacked Tristan when we were free. I chased him around the pen. I lashed out at him with my teeth and my hooves. I was so upset at what had happened.

In my attack mode, I whinnied, "Why did you do this? How could you hurt Fire Horse?"

Tristan cried back, "I am so sorry. I panicked. I didn't see her, and then I felt something underneath my legs. I thought I was being attacked, so I continued to rear in self-defense. I also love Fire Horse. I didn't mean to hurt her. I am sorry."

I realized that he had not done this intentionally. It was an unfortunate accident—a true calamity. We each felt terrible, and we sulked off to our respective corners of the enclosure.

It seemed like an eternity since I had last seen Fire Horse. I had not seen her in over a week. I knew from listening to people around the ranch that she had survived this horrific accident but that she had fractured her spine and had internal injuries too. I did not know what this meant. I had all sorts of stressful thoughts. *Would she return? Would she ever ride again? Would she still love horses? Would she still love me?* My spirit was broken.

One morning a few weeks after the accident, my spirit was restored. I saw her chestnut hair flowing in the wind as Fire Horse approaching my stall. Blaze and I whinnied with delight. She walked gingerly—but she walked. She smiled at me. I think I smiled back. I was so happy to see her. She walked into my stall and gave me a big hug. "I have missed you," she exclaimed. Blaze was nickering to her from his adjacent stall. She left momentarily and gave a big hug to Blaze too. When she returned, she told me that we wouldn't be riding for a while. She explained that she had a fractured back and some organ damage but that she would be better in short time. "I am relying on you, JJ, to help me through this," she said. *Of course*, I thought. *I would do anything for her.*

Over the course of the summer, Fire Horse and I began a disciplined routine of ground driving work. She would put long lines on me, and she would walk with me for hours each day. As she became stronger, we moved from just walking to me trotting and cantering "in her hand" while she walked behind me in the arena and around the ranch. I was happy to know that she was growing stronger. After a few months' time, we started working on our liberty routine again, and then one day at the end of that summer, she climbed onto my back and took me for a ride around the arena. I knew in that moment that she would be well again and I would remain her loyal horse.

ANOTHER MISHAP

    As autumn approached, Fire Horse was strong enough to ride, and we were preparing for another day of the horse event. But just one week before the event, another mishap was bestowed upon us. I needed new shoes, and my regular farrier was unable to shoe me. We used a local horse shoer, and it was disastrous. He accidentally stuck me with a hot nail inside my hoof wall, and he trimmed me so short I could barely walk. By the next morning, I was so sore I could not walk at all. We were not going to be in any show this year! Fire Horse had a specialist work on my feet. He made me a new set of shoes to remove the pressure, but my feet were beyond repair. It would take months for my feet to grow out, and I was abscessing where the hot nail had been misguided. I was in excruciating pain. Fire Horse treated my feet with a poultice and soaked my feet daily to provide pain relief. She gave me an anti-inflammatory too, but I could still scarcely walk. The veterinarian told her that it would be several months before I could resume any type of work. He suggested turnout in a grassy pasture and wrapped feet (with no shoes) until I was fully healed. It seemed that we would be rehabilitating together.

Fire Horse found me a grassy pasture a few miles away. She decided it would be best to keep me there while my feet recovered. The farm was beautiful, with rolling grass hills and a large pond. It was hundreds of acres in size with two jumping arenas, trails, a covered arena, and a round pen. The day she moved me was hard on everyone. I was leaving Tristan and Blaze behind, and I had no idea when I would see them next. I whinnied my goodbyes as we headed down the road in the trailer. I knew that I would be safe with Fire Horse, and she assured me that I would have great care at this farm. Then she added, "JJ, when you are better, we will have grassy fields filled with jumps that we can use and trails that we can ride on together. We will love it here." I was placed in a large, rolling pasture with an older white Arabian horse named Gus. I let him know that even though I was lame, I would still be the head horse in the pasture. He put up a bit of a fuss, but then he agreed. Many other pastures filled with young fillies and colts surrounded my pasture. It reminded me of my childhood days. This would be a peaceful place to be while my feet healed.

Over the first few weeks while I was at my new farm, Fire Horse went back and forth to take care of me and Blaze. I know she was also working many hours now that summer had ended. One day she came to the pasture, she was sad. I sensed this in her as she approached the pasture. I met her at the gate and wrapped my head around hers—my equivalent of a horse hug. "How do you always know what I am feeling?" she asked. I wish I could answer her. *I just did. I always knew what she was feeling. It was as though I could stare into her eyes and into her heart and soul.* She told me that Blaze had been given to an older woman who worked at the ranch where we had spent the last two summers. "JJ, I know she will take good care of Blaze. Her horse recently died, and she needed a good horse. Blaze is very happy there, and he will be a good horse for her. I know she will love him dearly. She told me I can still ride him or visit him anytime I want, but I'll miss having him in my daily life," Fire Horse added. I knew that Fire Horse was filled with sadness. I stood by her and hugged her. I too would miss seeing Blaze.

JUAN

It was several months into my rehabilitation, and I could now walk on soft ground with little discomfort. Fire Horse still wrapped my feet daily, as I had several abscesses that had moved down through my hoof walls over the past few months. The vet had told her that it would be a few more shoeing cycles (several months) before I could resume work. I knew that Fire Horse was growing anxious to ride me again. She rode Blaze and Tristan on occasion and also some of the horses at the farm. I often watched with envy whenever I would see her with another horse. But I also knew that we would be back to our routine shortly.

One afternoon, I saw Fire Horse heading up the hill with a steel gray horse. He looked familiar. I recognized that long, flowing mane—it was Juan! She brought Juan to the pasture and turned him out with me. "JJ, we have a new addition to our family, " she said to me as she turned him loose into the pasture with me. "Hooray!" I whinnied excitedly. Juan and I played for hours. We nipped at each other playfully. We wrestled our necks and rolled in the dirt like two young colts. It was just like old times. I had not realized that I had been so lonely for a playmate!

While my feet finished healing, Fire Horse started working with Juan. She worked with him doing all the liberty work that she had done with me in the past. She started to ground drive him, and she also would ride him in the arena. I watched them from a distance, and I often worried about her. He wasn't sure-footed like I was.

One day as they were coming down a steep hill on the trails around the farm, I saw Juan in the distance lose his footing. They fell together. I was worried, and I whinnied across the fields, "Are you okay?" But they couldn't hear me. Juan and Fire Horse got up quickly, and no one appeared hurt. *What a relief!* When Juan returned to the pasture, Fire Horse came in with him and approached me. "JJ," she said, "I think I will need your help in bringing Juan along. He doesn't seem to know where his feet are on some of the steeper trails. When you are well, I am going to ask you to help me pony him around the trails so that he can find his confidence." *Of course I would do that! I would do anything for Fire Horse.* She gave me a big hug and added, "JJ, you know I love Juan, but you will always be my special horse." She didn't need to tell me, because I already knew that I had a special place in her heart.

Over the next few weeks, I returned to light work. It was great to be out with Fire Horse again. Once I was back to full physical activity, Fire Horse and I began to pony Juan around the property. We traversed up and down the hilly trails until he became confident and sure-footed. We also worked in the arena together, and he would follow me over jumps. As time went by, Juan became a very capable trail horse. Juan thanked me for helping him one day.

"Thanks, JJ, " he said, "I was always afraid of the steep down hills. I would try to run down them to get it over as quickly as possible. Now I can take my time and just enjoy the scenery."

I nickered back as I ate my hay, "You are quite welcome. Just keep Fire Horse safe when she is under your care."

I really liked Juan and was happy to see his self-assuredness grow. But his newfound confidence had its consequences. As he grew stronger and more self-assured, he liked to challenge me for my lead position in the herd. I had to put this notion to rest immediately, and often he would get a quick warning and then a nip. He could be second in command, but I was the leader of the herd.

Juan and I grew to be great friends. We spent much time visiting as we grazed in the pasture. One day he asked me about my life and I shared with him my life on the track and my life with Fire Horse. I then asked him to tell me about his earlier life too. I knew that he and Tristan had been friends for quite some time, but I didn't know where he was born or what his life had been like before joining our family with Fire Horse. He went on to tell me his story.

"I was born on a warm, sunny day in May, and I am a Taurus Horse. I think this explains my affectionate nature and also why I like to be a part of a family. I am also quite fond of being groomed, and I am a bit food oriented. I think much of my nature is attributed to being born under the sign of Taurus.

"I was born in the southern part of the country where it is mostly flat. This is the reason why it was so hard for me to get my footing on the hilly terrain out here in the West. Like you, I was bred from parents of different breeds. My mother was a Quarter Horse, and like your mother, she was very kind and loving. I lived with her in a pasture for several months until I was weaned. I never met my father, but my mother told me he was a handsome Andalusian stallion. She told me I look just like him. When I was born, my coat was almost fully black, but as the years have passed, my coat turned a silver color.

"I grew up on a small farm with a very loving family. Much like Blaze, I always had children around. I really do enjoy youngsters! I would carry them bareback all over the pastures and into the surrounding orchards. They would come and play with me each day. They often spent hours grooming my mane and tail, and brushing my coat until I was rabbit soft.

"My training started when I was three years old. Just think, by that age you had already retired from racing! Mine was a much kinder start than yours. The family who raised me introduced my training to me, and I had complete trust in them. They gently introduced me to the saddle and bit. My initial work was just riding around on flat trails in the orchards and minding the children.

"As I turned four, they started me in dressage training with a local trainer. Like you, I found the constraint to be challenging. I was often lunged on side reins to help me with collection, but I much preferred to be out on the farm with the children. After I had a little basic dressage training, I was placed up for sale. I cannot tell you the emotions I felt. I had thought I would be with this family for the rest of my life. I couldn't imagine what I had done wrong. I was deeply saddened to know that I would be separated from these kind people and their children.

"Eventually a very nice woman came to buy me. You met her at the horseman's clinic. She owned me until she sold me to Fire Horse. When at first I was sold to her, I was heartbroken to leave my family, but I soon realized that I would be going to an exceptional home with a loving family. The woman who bought me also had two children. I immediately became the adored family horse, and I grew to love them immediately. I really enjoyed being with this woman. She was my southern Belle. We spent several years living on her family plantation in the South. One day her family relocated out West and she had me shipped out here in a large semi truck. I must say, I have never traveled in such luxury. I had a full-size stall in the truck, and I even had air conditioning !

"When I arrived at the new ranch in the West, Spirit Horse greeted me. She acquainted Belle and me with my new home. I was now to live out in a pasture with other horses on the rolling hills of a beautiful ranch. It was there that Tristan befriended me. He was my pasture mate, and he took very good care of me. When we went for trail rides, he led the way. When we were in pasture, he shared his hay. In those days, he was the dominant horse on the property, much like you are today. We became very good friends and played together for hours each day, much like you and I do these days.

"Spirit Horse introduced Belle to natural horsemanship, and that is how we ended up at the clinic where I met you. Belle and Spirit Horse had enrolled for a nine-day class, and as you know, I stayed for the whole summer. Unfortunately, Belle had prior plans to be on vacation with her family, and she missed much of the clinic. So while you and Fire Horse had the chance to work on trust, when we got to the liberty work, I was without Belle. Instead, you may recall, the horseman's apprentice worked with me. So while was I taught the same things you were, I never went through that same process with Belle. In fact, it has only been recently that I have started working on those things with Fire Horse, and I can already feel the trust growing between us. I know I'll never have quite the same place in her heart as you do, but I know that Fire Horse will grow to love me too.

"After the clinic ended and we left the horseman's ranch, I went into a training program. I don't think it suited me very well. Belle was still interested in trail riding, but she also wanted to go out on hunts with the hounds. I honestly don't think that I was the right horse for her anymore. On the hunts I was so fearful that I often galloped at full speed and wasn't sure-footed enough to handle the jumping courses. As you know, I had never been very sure-footed on the hilly trail system in this area either. Eventually Belle found herself another horse. I was heartbroken, of course, but I also knew that her new horse was better suited for the tasks at hand. I stayed with Belle and her family for a while longer, but I knew I would eventually part company with her family. This deeply saddened me, and I grew thin with worry.

"One day Belle arrived with her trailer. When she walked into the pasture, I knew immediately that I would be going to a new home that day. I was filled with sadness, and I think she was too. I had no idea where we were going. When we arrived, I was relieved to see a familiar face. Fire Horse thanked Belle for bringing me over and told Belle that she would give me a good home. I was still quite anxious. Fire Horse brought me to the grooming area and tried to spend some time grooming me. I was so filled with grief that I actually began to shake. Fire Horse tried to console me, but she realized that there was little she could do for me in that moment. She assured me that I would have a good life with her. She gave me some treats and then she walked me up the hill to this pasture. It was then that I realized I would be living with you. I was so happy to see you that day. You may recall that we played like young colts that afternoon.

"Since that time, I have grown more confident and I have put on weight and muscle. Thanks to you and Fire Horse, I feel much more sure-footed, and I have confidence on the trails and in jumping obstacles. I know that Fire Horse has promised me a home for the rest of my days. There is great comfort in knowing that I am part of a family and will never be sold again. I really do enjoy my new life with you and Fire Horse. But I also know that you are her special horse, and I wish that I could be that special horse for someone too."

I softened toward Juan that afternoon as I realized we would be brothers for the remainder of our lives. I offered some kind words to him, "Juan, I am happy that you are in our family. I know I am Fire Horse's special horse, but she loves you too. You need not worry. You too will be the special horse for someone. Just trust me." With that we made a pact to be *fire brothers*, which I believe is far better than blood brothers.

AN OLD FRIEND IS LOST AND ANOTHER IS FOUND

The next year went by quickly. Juan and I had become good friends, and we played together daily in our pasture. Spirit Horse often came to the farm and rode Juan, and sometimes we would go out to the beach or to a local park for a ride. Juan became a reliable mount, and I knew Fire Horse enjoyed having both of us in her life. Fire Horse was healed, and so was I. We were a happy family.

Over the years, Fire Horse and I had grown quite close. I could read her emotions clearly, and she too was in touch with my feelings and energies. One afternoon she arrived with great sadness upon her. I had sensed her presence before I had even seen her. I waited for her by the pasture gate. When she saw me, her eyes welled up tears. She came into the pasture and wrapped her arms around me. I knew she had suffered a great loss. Just as she told me what had happened, I saw the image. Blaze had passed away in his sleep the previous night. Fire Horse was filled with grief. I knew that Blaze was a gentle soul and that his kind spirit would live on in many. I too felt the loss of his great and loving presence. We stood for a long time together. Eventually Juan wandered over too, and we all stood quietly together in the pasture. It was our extended memorial to Blaze.

Within a few days of this terrible loss, I was surprised to see another old friend. Fire Horse was leading an older chestnut up the hill toward my pasture. I hardly recognized him. His head was hanging down to his knees, and he looked depressed. When Fire Horse got to the gate, I recognized that the horse was Tristan. I whinnied, "Tristan. Welcome!" Juan also whinnied a greeting to our old friend. Tristan's ears perked up. We galloped to the gate to greet him. Fire Horse led him into the pasture and let him free. The three of us ran around the field and celebrated our reunion. Spirit Horse and Fire Horse watched us play for nearly an hour. They also looked pleased to see us all back together again. We asked Tristan how he had been. "I have been good, but then I lost my dearest friend the other day. I have been grief-stricken by the loss of Blaze." We nuzzled him. "We know. We miss Blaze too," we replied. We all stood quiet together and remembered our grand adventures with our great friend. Life would never be the same without Blaze. We made a pact that we would never forget him.

SOMATICS AND COUNTY FAIRS

Over the next several months, after Tristan reunited with the herd, life was very good. Fire Horse and I played together often. We would jump the obstacles in the jumping arena and in the cross-country field at the farm. The best part was that we jumped them at liberty — with no bridle. We both felt so free as we cantered though the fields with our respective chestnut manes flowing in the wind.

One day, we gave a demonstration to a group of schoolchildren who were visiting the farm. They were youngsters, and they all loved horses. Fire Horse sent me over the jumps from the ground and then, of course, after easily clearing them, I would canter back to her. One of the little girls asked if I was magic. Fire Horse said, "Yes, JJ is magic—at least for me!" The little girl smiled and said that she also wanted to have a magic horse! I really enjoyed these types of demonstrations. I especially liked when children were around. There was something special about the energy of a child. There was an element of creativity and playfulness in children that I rarely observed in adults. I was starting to understand why Blaze and Juan had been so captivated by the children in their lives.

One of the things that Fire Horse and I learned when we studied natural horsemanship was the use of "somatics" for releasing tension in horses. Equine somatics is similar in concept to yoga for horses. Fire Horse learned how to release all the tension in my muscles from a wise and gentle woman. For these attributes, I referred to her as Owl Horse. One day she asked Fire Horse if she and I would give a demonstration on using somatics with horses. "Of course," Fire Horse responded, " but I think we should also show JJ's movement at liberty before and after releasing tension in his muscles so that people can see the benefit for their own horses." It was agreed that we would give an equine somatics demonstration at the farm. I was excited to perform again!

On the day of our equine somatics demonstration, many people showed up to see us. Owl Horse and Spirit Horse narrated as Fire Horse sent me around the arena. I demonstrated all of my gaits—walk, trot, and canter—so they could see my natural movement. Then Fire Horse and I did our liberty routine on the ground. I cantered around her in a tight circle and toward her as she backed in various patterns, and then I moved sideways away from and toward her using just energy from her body. The audience was in awe as they watched. Then Fire Horse spent the next hour working on all of my muscles. She released the tension in my legs, shoulders, spine, head, and tail. I found this so relaxing that I found myself nearly sleeping. When we completed the muscle work, Fire Horse sent me around the arena again and then repeated the liberty work so that the audience could observe my improved flexibility and relaxation. We then saddled up and rode around the arena at liberty and went through a course of jumps without a bridle. Fire Horse next put a bridle on me to show my collected work. In my relaxed state, we performed a demonstration of leg yields and half pass with ease. At the end of our demonstration, everyone applauded. Fire Horse gave me a proud pat and gave me one of my favorite treats— a ripe banana. It was great to be in the "show ring" again.

That summer Owl Horse was invited to give a demonstration on equine somatics at the local county fair on the fourth of July weekend. Fire Horse and I would be the final show in the horse arena each evening. I was excited to know that we were going to have another adventure. The event was held at a large county fair with a full carnival. There were bands, crafts, farm animals, pig races, llama parades, and even a giant Ferris wheel. When I arrived, it reminded me a bit of Vegas!

Spirit Horse came with us and narrated the liberty work. Owl Horse narrated the somatic work. We gave our demonstration in the evening following the widely famous pig races in the barnyard adjacent to the arena. We had a large crowd with hundreds of people and many families with their children. I followed closely behind Fire Horse, and she brought me along the fence line to introduce me to the audience. We did the same routine that we had done for the somatics workshop. The families and children were astonished as they watched me do my liberty routine with Fire Horse. I received a grand applause as we cleared our last jump together. Fire Horse and I often stayed an additional hour each night just talking to all the interested people in the audience. My favorite part was being around the children. While Fire Horse spoke to the audience, I received numerous pats from my little fan club.

On our last night at the fair, a woman approached Fire Horse and commended her on the relationship she had with me. She said it had brought her to tears to watch us work together. She then told Fire Horse that there was another woman who worked with equine-guided leadership and education and that we should seek her out. Fire Horse took down the information and said she would contact that woman. I wondered — *could this be yet another adventure for us?*

THE HORSE PSYCHIC

One sunny afternoon, I did not see Fire Horse, but I was "contacted by her" through a horse psychic. Juan, Tristan, and I had been sunbathing and taking our afternoon snooze when out of the blue an image of Fire Horse came into my mind. Somehow images and questions were being presented to me. I thought at first that I was dreaming. But then it became clear to me that I was being contacted by an animal communicator — a horse psychic! At first, the horse psychic asked me what I liked to do best. I sent an image of me jumping over the large cross-country jumps in the fields. She asked me to give her an image of myself and asked that I describe myself. I had to ponder for a moment as I thought about the best way to describe myself.

I conveyed to her that I was smart, good-looking, athletic, and a leader. I also communicated to her that I could be a prankster or trickster—it was my coyote medicine— I had a good sense of humor! I sent an image of my "stallion-like" self with my beautiful glossy chestnut coat and I presented myself playing with my pasture mates—but clearly leading, and then jumping complicated obstacles with Fire Horse by my side. I was asked if I liked to do my demonstrations with Fire Horse. "Of course," I responded. I presented an image of me cantering behind Fire Horse and doing one of our liberty presentations. I conveyed the happiness that I felt to the horse psychic. Finally, I was asked if there was anything else that I would like to share with Fire Horse.

"Yes, please tell Fire Horse that I make her look good! Tell her that when we are doing our demonstrations together that it is 80 percent me and 20 percent her!" Of course, I knew we were a team—but I thought that Fire Horse would appreciate my humor in this last message!

EQUINE-GUIDED EDUCATION

A few months after our performance at the county fair, Fire Horse contacted the woman who specialized in equine-guided education. Fire Horse informed me that we were going to do a clinic with her. When we arrived at her ranch, I immediately liked the energy. It felt calm and yet alive. There were many horses, mostly mares, living out in pasture together on the rolling hills of the ranch. There were cattle and goats also grazing in adjacent pastures. I was turned out into a large sand arena with a beautiful vista of the ranch.

Shortly after we arrived at the ranch, Fire Horse went off to check in for the clinic, and she turned me out in the arena to stretch my legs. I rolled in the sand and then went to the pasture side of the arena so that I could introduce myself to the horses in the abutting pasture. Many horses from the pasture came up and welcomed me. Lacy and her daughter Jet Star arrived first, then Stella and Superman. Lacy was the herd leader, and she told me that they all belonged to a woman named Eagle Horse. I introduced myself, and explained that I was also the herd leader in my pasture back home and that I was here with Fire Horse.

I asked them about this equine-guided work that we were here to study. Lacy explained to me that we would work with people to help guide them in their life.

"How?" I asked.

"You will see," responded Lacy.

She then explained Eagle Horse was very intuitive and worked with all sorts of people using horses. She used horses as guides in leadership workshops and in coaching people to discover their innermost dreams and goals. Lacy explained that Eagle Horse had tuned into the intuitive aspect of the horse and that she could read horse body language easily. Our job was easy, she explained — we would just be ourselves. We would respond to the energy and body language that a person would bring to us. She explained that Eagle Horse would often ask people that she was coaching a series of questions or ask them to make a declaration about some aspect of their life. Lacy further explained to me that as horses, we would easily read the person's energy and emotion. It would be easy for us to determine if the person was being authentic, that is, if their words matched their true feelings. Lacy explained that our work was just to use our natural intuitive abilities and in doing so, we could help people overcome their deepest fears or realize their inner aspirations. I knew that I was very intuitive. For years I had read Fire Horse's emotions and energy. It seemed that now I would learn to use my intuitive abilities to help others. This was very exciting to me.

Over the next several months, Fire Horse and I worked continuously with Eagle Horse. Fire Horse learned to tap into her intuitive side. Fire Horse already knew that she had a spiritual connection to me, but she grew to realize that she also had ability for energetic communication with horses. Fire Horse had already mentored many people in her life, and she was a skilled horsewoman, so this pursuit would be a natural venue for her. We learned to work with people in a round pen environment, to work with leading exercises, and to utilize creative exercises that could enable people to find their inner paths. For example, one day we set up a complicated obstacle course in the arena. I watched as Jet Star and the man working with her navigated the challenge. The obstacles were meant to symbolize the obstacles in the path of his goals. He was then asked to navigate the course with Jet Star and lead the horse through the obstacles. Such obstacles might include small jumps, bridges, rails, cones, etc. The challenge was that he couldn't pull the horse through. Instead, the horse had to walk by his side. The horse had to believe in his ability to overcome the obstacle. That is, he had to find it in himself to believe that he could overcome the various obstacles in his way to accomplishing his goals. In the human analogy, a jump might represent a financial obstacle in starting one's own business, for example. When he found his inner confidence and he believed in himself, the horse readily navigated the course with him. The outcome of the exercise was that he had found it in himself to believe that he could overcome all the obstacles that stood between him and his personal goal. It was an amazing sight to watch.

Over the course of a year, Fire Horse completed her studies with Eagle Horse and became a certified equine-guided educator. I was to be her partner. Through this process, Fire Horse and I had more opportunities to participate in the public forum. At the Annual Meeting for Equine-Guided Educators, we gave a demonstration that coupled the natural horsemanship, somatics, and energy work. The audience enjoyed watching us go through our liberty work without any tools—just energy communication and body language. As always, I had fun playing by Fire Horse's side. As a result of my various experiences, I was invited to go with Eagle Horse to the Western States Horse Exposition to give a three-day demonstration on intuitive horsemanship. Fire Horse and Juan came with me, and even Juan had a chance to do some of this work too. Alongside Eagle Horse, I worked with many people, ranging from children to older adults, who had come to the exposition to learn more about horses and intuitive horsemanship. I would walk by their side as they made declarations about interests in their lives or goals that they wanted to achieve. It was easy for me to read the energy and alignment of this energy with their spoken words. When the energy was positive and authentic, I found myself walking by their side with ease, but when the words and energies didn't match, I found myself disinterested in partnering with that person. My response to the various people enabled Eagle Horse to give constructive feedback to the people. I learned that many people don't realize that their spoken word often doesn't match their real feelings. It was a successful venue, and at the end I felt quite good about this work.

Once Fire Horse had completed her equine-guided education certification, we began to work with people together. At first we focused on working with doctoral students from the university and horse friends who knew Fire Horse. We offered many practice sessions, and I learned much as I worked with each of these individuals. Juan was included in our coaching work, and I noticed that many people gravitated toward him because of his very kind spirit. I found myself proud to be Juan's friend and partner, and not the least bit envious. Maybe I too was becoming a better horse.

One day, Fire Horse and I worked with a young woman who was struggling with self-esteem. When Fire Horse asked her what she would like to work on, she told Fire Horse that she felt as though she had not done enough in her life. She was struggling with self-worth. Fire Horse asked her to make a positive declaration about herself and to then have me walk by her side. The young woman worked on her declaration. Fire Horse asked her to say it out loud and to believe it in her body. She explained that when her inner feelings matched her words, that I would readily walk by her side. The young woman made her declaration, "I am enough. I am worthy." But I didn't feel that her energy matched her words. Instead I felt her self-doubt about these positive words. She walked off, and I stayed where I was. Fire Horse had her try again, but again I felt the conflict and could not follow her. Fire Horse asked her to speak about something that she was truly proud of in her life. The young woman told her of an accomplishment in her life for which she felt proud. Fire Horse asked her to state out loud that she was proud of this accomplishment and to feel it in her body. She asked her to take me for a walk with this energy. As the young woman made her new declaration, I felt her positive energy. She was authentic with her words and her emotion. I easily walked by her side, as I felt aligned with this positive energy. We spent the afternoon building up a series of proud accomplishments until the young woman truly felt worthy of her life. In the end, I was able to walk by her side with her initial declaration. The young woman was beaming with pride when we finished our session. She thanked Fire Horse profusely and then gave me a big hug. It felt great to be a part of such a transformation.

Eventually, Fire Horse printed cards with the name Fire Horse Life Coaching. She placed a picture of me jumping on the front and a picture of Juan on the backside. She then printed flyers entitled "Empowerment through Horses" and posted them locally. As a result, we had the chance to work with young people seeking to improve self-esteem, and others to find direction for professional growth or balance in their lives. We worked with people looking to make career changes or those who were looking to find their inner selves. Together, Fire Horse, Juan, and I worked with many people. Many of these people made declarations for change in their life. Fire Horse worked with the people until their visions and goals felt real for them. I really enjoy this type of work. Together with Fire Horse, we make a great team.

THE HERD EXPANDS

One winter day, Fire Horse arrived with another person —
a man! I knew immediately that this man was not here for
life coaching. Somehow Fire Horse was different around him.
When they approached the pasture, I sensed her nervousness.
I immediately came to the gate and made my presence known.
I placed myself between Fire Horse and this visitor. He offered
to pet me, but I pinned my ears — she was mine! On my side,
Juan came up and greeted this man. Unlike me, Juan liked
him immediately. "We'll have to see about this," I nickered
to Juan.

I had often found myself envious when Fire Horse
diverted her full attention away from me. Sometimes, this was

a conversation with Spirit Horse or her working with Juan instead of me. I sometimes made a raucous noise to get her full attention. Fire Horse has told me that she is fully aware that this is my intention, and she has always reminded me that I am her kindred spirit. Yet somehow I felt jealous when this man arrived.

We all went to the arena together. Fire Horse let Juan and me canter around the arena. Then she did her liberty routine with me. I gave my best performance so that this man could see how special I was to Fire Horse. But he stood at the other end of the arena and patted Juan, who was already smitten with him. *Who was this guy?*

We went back to the grooming area. Fire Horse groomed me and then showed this man how to groom Juan. He spoke gently to Juan, and Juan was clearly at ease with him. As Fire Horse saddled me, I tried to get a read on this man. He was kind. He was authentic. He clearly had a sense of humor. But I sensed that he could be a trickster. He had coyote medicine in him, just as I did. I decided I would call him Coyote Horse. Clearly Fire Horse was smitten with him too. *I would have to keep an eye on him.*

We went to the arena and Fire Horse rode me without a bridle, and she took me over a course of jumps too. I gave my best effort. Coyote Horse needed to see that Fire Horse and I were kindred spirits. He smiled as he watched. Juan had not left his side through all of this, and then Coyote Horse asked if he could ride Juan. I thought, *This should be something to watch.* He got on Juan bareback. I thought Juan might get nervous, but instead he seemed at ease. After Fire Horse and I finished our ride, we joined Juan and Coyote Horse for a leisurely walk around the arena. As Juan approached I pinned my ears, but Juan knew that my warning was not meant for him.

When Juan and I returned to the pasture, I asked him, "What can you tell me about Coyote Horse?"

Juan replied, "He is a very nice man. I liked the way that he groomed me and spoke to me." Juan told me that Coyote Horse was genuine and that he loved nature, animals, and horses.

I added my thoughts, "Well, I think he is interested in our Fire Horse!"

Juan nickered happily, "He is, but you shouldn't feel threatened. You know that Fire Horse is your special person, and I have this sense that Coyote Horse is going to be my kindred spirit." I was somewhat relieved. I knew that Juan was entitled to have a kindred spirit too.

As the months went by, it became clear that Coyote Horse was going to be a part of our herd. We often went out on long trail rides together, Fire Horse on me and Coyote Horse on Juan. I thought this wasn't going to be so bad after all. Then one day Fire Horse told me that she and Coyote Horse were going to be married. At first I sulked, but she reminded me that nothing would change between us, and that I would always be paramount in her heart. As time went by, I grew to accept the union of Coyote Horse and Fire Horse. He made her happy, and she deserved happiness. Juan too had his kindred spirit. I decided that I, too, was content with my expanded family.

Fire Horse and Coyote Horse married in Africa. It seemed that they were gone forever. Weeks went by, and I started to wonder if she would ever return. Fire Horse had told me that they were going on a horseback safari in Africa. It was almost more than I could bear—not only was she in another country with Coyote Horse, but she was riding other horses too! I found myself anxious for her return.

Spirit Horse took care of me while Fire Horse was away. She often tried to reassure me. "JJ, Fire Horse will be home soon. You know she loves you, and she is thinking about you. This marriage is a good thing. Coyote Horse is a good match for her," she said as she groomed me. As the weeks went by, I grew grumpy. I knew Spirit Horse was almost as eager as I was for the return of Fire Horse. When Fire Horse arrived back home, I immediately felt her presence. She was sending me her thoughts. I knew she had missed me too! My mood immediately perked up.

When Fire Horse returned, she indulged me with praise and carrots. We resumed our life coaching work. Fire Horse took me out on trails with Spirit Horse and Coyote Horse. We even started to work on dressage again. By this time, Fire Horse had found a trainer who shared in her love of horses and in bringing out the best in horses. She believed in riding with seat and legs and very soft hands. She was consistent with my prior natural horsemanship training. Best of all, she loved chestnuts and Thoroughbreds! I found it easy to work in self-carriage with her tutelage. Fire Horse and I had finally found a way to enjoy dressage together. This trainer had much praise for me and always had sweet treats for me too. I decided I would call her Candy Horse. Life was returning to normal again—*well, at least as normal as it could be.*

One day Fire Horse was ground driving me around the property, and I knew she did not feel well. Finally she sat down, frustrated with her own exhaustion. "What is wrong with me, JJ?" she asked. I walked slowly toward her and rested my muzzle on her stomach and gently rubbed up and down. I looked deeply into her eyes with mine. My knowing eyes told her something that she had not yet known. She was expecting a filly. "I can't be, can I?" she pondered out loud. I looked at her with my deep and knowing eyes to assure her she was in fact going to have a little filly. She hugged me. Fire Horse had wanted a child for as long as I had known her. Fire Horse was ecstatic by the news, but I also knew that soon many people would be advising her to not ride horses. I let her know that I would keep her and this filly safe when they were in my charge.

I was true to my word. When we went out for trail rides, I kept the pace extra slow, and I walked gingerly up and down the hills. I did not let Tristan or Juan lead when we went out for trail rides together. Fire Horse told me that she had full confidence in me. Fire Horse told me that the filly's name would be Savanna to reflect her African origins. I assured Fire Horse that I would always keep her and Savanna Filly safe.

Over the next several months, Tristan, Juan, Gus, and I checked in with Fire Horse each time she arrived in the pasture to check on our little filly. Each day we saw Fire Horse, we would place our muzzles on her and offered our various greetings to Savanna Filly. We all agreed that it was nice to have a little filly in the herd.

LIFE IS GOOD

I don't know what the future holds, but I do know that my life to date has been quite good. Just as my mother had told me long ago, I was not destined for a life as a racehorse but rather an adventurous life closely weaved with people. Looking back on my life, I have learned many things. I have learned that our true friends see our beauty within and do not judge us on our exterior. I have learned that sometimes things happen to us for reasons that we don't yet understand and that we must trust in the unknown. We each have our own unique offerings in this world and to be our best, we must simply walk in our own unique hoof prints.

I know that I have been fortunate to have many great equine and human friends in my life. I cannot imagine what my life would have been like if Fire Horse had not seen my inner beauty and potential many years ago when I was still a gangly colt. Fire Horse believed in me when no one else did, and she never gave up on me throughout all of our various struggles. I have had many great adventures with Fire Horse, and I look forward to growing old with her and my extended herd.

www.ingramcontent.com/pod-product-compliance
Lightning Source LLC
Chambersburg PA
CBHW061305280526
45784CB00002B/900